SLAY LIKE A GIRL

Ditch the Demons and Be Your Own Hero

Micol Ostow

Running Press
PHILADELPHIA

Running Press
Hachette Book Group
1290 Avenue of the Americas, New York, NY 10104
www.runningpress.com
@Running_Press

Printed in China

First Edition: October 2019

Published by Running Press, an imprint of Perseus Books, LLC, a subsidiary of Hachette Book Group, Inc. The Running Press name and logo is a trademark of the Hachette Book Group.

The Hachette Speakers Bureau provides a wide range of authors for speaking events. To find out more, go to www.hachettespeakersbureau.com or call (866) 376-6591.

The publisher is not responsible for websites (or their content) that are not owned by the publisher.

Print book cover design by Frances J. Soo Ping Chow and interior design by Corinda Cook.

Library of Congress Control Numher: 2019943571

ISBNs: 978-0-7624-6838-6 (flexibound), 978-0-7624-6840-9 (ebook)

RRD-S

10 9 8 7 6 5 4 3 2 1

Contents

INTRODUCTION

BUFFY: I mean . . . I guess everyone's alone. But being a Slayer? There's a burden we can't share.

FAITH: And no one else can feel it. Thank god we're hot chicks with superpowers.

BUFFY: Takes the edge off.

—**"End of Days"**

When it debuted in the nineties, *Buffy the Vampire Slayer* turned tired, sexist tropes on their head and introduced a truly empowered heroine to fans who were more than ready to meet her. The show's cultural relevance is strong as ever, with a fresh wave of fans finding their way to the show in the wake of its recent twentieth anniversary. So who better than Buffy and company to teach today's nasty woman (and her allies) how to slay her personal demons?

BUFFY: AN ORIGIN STORY

When *Buffy the Vampire Slayer*—based on the movie of the same name—premiered in 1997, no one could have predicted how influential the show (and its eponymous heroine) would become. A handful of savvier critics recognized it at the time for its "deliciously funny satirical gore," but for every enthusiastic media response, there was a dubious source like the *New York Times*, who declared, "Nobody is likely to take this oddball camp exercise seriously, though the violence can get decidedly creepy."

As Buffy herself might say, *Wrong much?* Not about the creep factor, of course; that stayed high—and awesome—throughout the series, but about the ways in which we, as an audience and a media culture, were good and ready to take a show like *Buffy* seriously. And with good reason: Buffy creator Joss Whedon took the outdated horror movie paradigm of the Final Girl and gave her a modern, feminist twist. As *Bitch* magazine pointed out, "Before *Buffy*, [horror stories] focused primarily on the male monster antagonists who preyed on . . . nubile young things." Whedon has said in interviews how weary he'd grown of movies where "bubbleheaded blondes wandered into dark alleys and got murdered by some creature."

He wasn't the only one.

This subversion of trope was welcomed by viewers; rather than warn the imperiled girl to beware the danger down the dark alley, *Buffy* fans cheered on the Slayer while she stalked her prey. As *Bitch* went on to tell us, "Instead of shouting, *Don't go in there!* to the naïve gal traipsing through the darkened vacant house, we shout, *Go, girl!* as Buffy enters the dark alley to dispatch the monster of the moment."

So, precisely how did we get from watching bubbleheaded blondes wandering foolishly down dark alleys to the feisty, fearless young woman whose birthright it became to hunt monsters in the very same dark corners we helpless females were taught to assiduously avoid? Read on.

FIRST THINGS LAST: SLASHER MOVIES, THE FINAL GIRL, AND BUFFY

> "I'm Buffy, and you're . . . history!"
>
> —Buffy, "Never Kill a Boy on the First Date"

You've seen the movie: the one with the babysitter being stalked by her deranged brother (*Halloween*).*

Or, fast-forward to the eighties and the one with the girl being tormented in her dreams by a real-life nightmare stalker (*Nightmare on Elm Street*).

Historically, girls in horror movies were victims first and foremost. Traditionally, in these movies, females were victims of violence (often sexualized) more frequently than males; their onscreen fear, suffering, and eventual death was more prolonged than that of their male counterparts; and violence against women was more often linked to sexual activity.

That was then.

And now?

Enter the Final Girl.

First formally introduced by Carol J. Clover in her 1992 book, *Men, Women, and Chain Saws: Gender in the Modern Horror Film*, the Final Girl as a trope and archetype had a more limited definition than the one we know more colloquially today. In horror movies (and in slasher movies in particular), the Final Girl is the last victim standing, the one who gets to confront the killer at the movie's end. According to Clover, within the genre, viewers generally began the movie in the point of view of the killer, but by the movie's end, we'd been recentered around the Final Girl's perspective. In a genre known for being unabashedly male-centric, this was huge. Clover looked specifically at slasher

---

*(Don't worry—she gets another, more satisfying crack at him in the 2018 sequel; Buffy's not the only scream queen who evolved for contemporary audiences.)

movies from the seventies and eighties where the Final Girl was "allowed" to survive the threat of the male gaze thanks to her moral purity.

(Remember Randy's "rules one must abide by in order to successfully survive a horror movie" rant in *Scream?* You can't drink, do drugs, or have sex—and this applies twofold to a Final Girl. Basically, she's a major buzzkill. And for her troubles, she gets to live.)

Originally, too, it was common for a Final Girl to be brunette (gasp! the horror!) and to have a more "masculine" or androgynous name. Though a classic Final Girl will survive a monster attack by her own wits and grit, she's ultimately rescued by a male authority figure (think Laurie Strode being saved by Dr. Sam Loomis in *Halloween*).

As slasher films rose to new heights of popularity in the eighties, so-called "scream queen" heroines were eventually (maybe even some-what reluctantly) allowed a few imperfections; *A Nightmare on Elm Street*'s Nancy may have been "purer" than her friend Tina, but she was hardly chaste . . .

The Girls were also, at long last, allowed to triumph at the movie's end on their own. (Though it's telling that *Elm Street* was one of many more "progressive" postmodern horror movies to offer an empowered Final Girl a decidedly ambiguous ending, where we, the audience, aren't sure if the monster has truly been vanquished.)

For decades, pop-horror told us that women only fight back as a desperate, reluctant last resort and only within the context of the male gaze. *Buffy* undid all of that with a single premise:

What if the blonde girl being chased down the dark alley was actually a superhero?

What if she fought back *as her destiny*, her calling, on behalf of humankind?

What if she and her extended cadre of badass female warriors tapped into their collective strength together to save the world repeatedly?

And what if, in the process of gender-bending, genre-flipping, and all-out kicking ass, she *got. It. Done?*

What then?

Buffy offered up a theory or two.

JUST A GRRRL: THE NINETIES

As horror movies evolved and transformed from the eighties into the nineties and the turn of the millennium, other corners of media and pop culture were also reshaping themselves. Specifically, in the early nineties, third-wave feminism was emerging as an ideology of its own. Its roots can be traced to the Riot Grrrl movement in the Pacific Northwest, a subset of punk culture where punk girls were rioting (get it?) against the sexism of their music and community.

Cyberculture, of course, had a big influence, too, as girls came online to find a new community of feminist e-zines, websites, and chat rooms available to them like never before. Like everything else, feminism suddenly had an instantly accessible global platform.

Critics of third-wave feminism often dismissed it as "girly" feminism because expressions of extreme femininity (as opposed to the rejection of traditional gender codes favored by radical feminists) were co-opted as a challenge to traditional patriarchal objectification of women. This new strand of an old movement asserted that women reclaiming agency over their clothing and aesthetic choices could only be seen as self-expression: *be gone, male gaze!*

Women could wear what they wanted to wear and behave as traditionally "femme" as they wanted to without inviting sexist stereotypes, assumptions, and attitudes. (Women had come a long way, baby. And they'd tell you all about it, wearing baby doll dresses paired with combat boots.)

The Spice Girls rose to stardom and wrapped female friendship, loyalty, and commercial domination into a fun, palatable package that consumers could drink up with a shiny pink straw. Gwen Stefani and No Doubt's smash hit "Just a Girl" gave a window into the female struggle, and Julia Stiles's portrayal of the feminist "shrew" in *10 Things I Hate About You*, an update of Shakespeare's *The Taming of the Shrew*, gave viewers a different kind of heroine than they were used to.

Grrrl power then became (say it with me now) GIRL POWER! And pop culture couldn't get enough of it.

From Daria Morgendorffer to Missy Elliott and the queens of nineties' hip-hop, from *Xena: Warrior Princess* to Hermione Granger, nineties' pop culture was all about sisters doing it for themselves (and their fellow sisters). Cue the 1995 launch of teen-programming mono-lith the WB network, which swooped in with a slate of quirky, distinctly teen-centric programming at a time when tween and teen spending power was soaring to new heights. *Buffy* premiered as a mid-season replacement on March 10, 1997. Initially written off as a punchline, the show was followed soon enough by other teen jugger-nauts like *Dawson's Creek*, *Charmed*, *Felicity*, and more, growing the WB—and later on, UPN—into destination networks for the young, hip, and in search of drama.

Buffy was the quintessential feminist archetype of that cultural moment: thin, white (intersectional feminism just beginning to flex its much-needed muscles), blonde, conventionally pretty, and not afraid to be girlie. Yes, she broke a nail while patrolling in season one, but that didn't stop her from thwarting the Master's prophecy.

> "We saved the world. I say we party. I mean, I got all pretty."
>
> —Buffy, "Prophecy Girl"

Though the show has rightly been critiqued for its lack of diversity, it's worth noting that *Buffy*, the show, was an important foundation for the inclusive feminist politics we strive to realize today. Before *Buffy*, female characters in media were often disposable. And female *superheroes*? As main characters? Try again.

Strong, outspoken, and stead-fastly unapologetic about her gender (and *definitely* not limited by being "just a girl," either), if Buffy was a stepping-stone for female protagonists of the postmillennial landscape, it's fair to say she was an indispensable one at that.

CHOSEN, FINALLY:
THE *BUFFY* BOTTOM LINE

So, back to our initial question, then: What if the Final Girl fights back? What if she *wins*? What if she's not "just" a girl at all but humankind's one salvation?

What if—after seven seasons of fighting innumerable Big Bads—she quit the Council of (mostly male) Watchers that created her, made her own rules, and empowered every other Slayer in the world with her full potential?

I hate that there's evil, and that I was chosen to fight it. I wish, a whole lot of the time, that I hadn't been. [. . .] But this isn't about wishes. This is about choices. I believe we can beat this evil. Not when it comes, not when its army is ready—now. Tomorrow morning I'm opening the seal. I'm going down into the hellmouth, and I'm finishing this once and for all.

Right now you're asking yourself, "What makes this different? What makes us any more than a bunch of girls?"

It's true none of you have the power that Faith and I do. So here's the part where you make a choice:

What if you could have that power now?

In every generation, one Slayer is born . . . because a bunch of men who died thousands of years ago made up that rule. They were powerful men. This woman is more powerful than all of them combined. So I say we change the rule. I say *my* power should be *our* power.

Tomorrow, Willow will use the essence of this scythe to change our destiny. From now on, every girl in the world who might be a Slayer, *will* be a Slayer. Every girl who could have the power . . . *will* have the power. *Can* stand up, *will* stand up. Slayers, every one of us.

Make your choice.

Are you ready to be strong?

—Buffy Summers, "Chosen"

If you read that and thought, *Heck, yeah*, come on in—the (holy) water's fine.

If the nineties, and *Buffy's* origins, were all about girl power, then we're living in an era of true feminist strength.

If the future is female, then *Buffy* is more relevant than ever.

And don't just take my word for it: comics, animation, new young adult, and even picture book lines speak to the cult icon's evergreen influence. Not to mention the fresh wave of fandom that found its way to the show in the wake of its recent twentieth anniversary.

Buffy isn't going anywhere. Feminist culture is loud and proud as ever. And thank goddess (as Willow would say) for that.

Buffy and her fellow babes— Willow, Cordelia, Anya, and more —have a lot to offer in terms of hilarious, quotable, pop-culture savvy insights, observations, and life lessons. Wanna werk like a Slayer? This is the book for you. It's your handbook to slaying like a girl—

the Buffy way. Because, after all, who better than Buffy and her fellow badass babes to teach us how to slay our personal demons with strength *and* style?

Have a seat, take a bite . . . the girls are glad you're here.

PART I:

THE BABES
OF *BUFFY*

BOY : How'd you do that? . . . You're just a girl.

BUFFY : That's what I keep saying.

—"The Gift"

Naturally, there'd be no discussion of *Buffy's* impact on girl power without a look at the women wielding that power themselves. Friends, frenemies, newfound sisters, and even a recovering magic addict and an ex- (or is that newly reinstated but still reformed?) demon count themselves among the Slayer's cohorts.*

*While we're aware—and thrilled—that the *Buffy* mythology lives on in various ongoing comics sequels and the television spin-off *Angel*, for our purposes we'll be focusing on the women of the "original-flavor" *Buffy*verse.

BUFFY ANNE SUMMERS

Needless to say, there'd be no *Buffy* to speak of without, well, Buffy.

> "Into every generation, a Slayer is born. One girl in all the world, a Chosen One."
>
> —Giles, "Welcome to the Hellmouth"

(Well . . . sort of. More on that later.)

Born in 1981 and called to Slaying in 1996 at fifteen, Buffy Summers (played to iconic perfection by Sarah Michelle Gellar) was initially a fairly reluctant superhero. Flashbacks revealed in season two show Buffy as she's first called, approached by an early Watcher as she happily basks in the sun on the steps of her L.A. high school, waiting for her latest boy toy to come pick her up.

FUN FACT: Sarah Michelle Gellar had auditioned for the role of Sabrina on *Sabrina, the Teenage Witch* before accepting the role of Buffy Summers.

WATCHER: There isn't much time. You must come with me. Your destiny awaits.

BUFFY: I don't have a destiny. I'm destiny-free, really.

WATCHER: Yes, you have. You are the Chosen One. You alone can stop them.

BUFFY: Who?

WATCHER: The Vampires.

BUFFY: Huh?

—"Becoming, Part 1"

We see her train, hesitantly, and slay her first vampire (also hesitantly albeit successfully). Eventually, she faces her demonic foes in a showdown that leads to her being forced to burn down her entire high school. Unsurprisingly, she's expelled from school, which is what prompts her mother, Joyce, to pick up stakes (no pun intended) to relocate to Sunnydale in search of a fresh start (and ideally a daughter who doesn't burn down high schools in a perfect world).

But a secret identity is, as Buffy herself says, "a thing of work" ("Welcome to the Hellmouth"); and in Sunnydale, there's no such thing as coincidence. Upon arriving at Sunnydale High, Buffy quickly learns that the school librarian, Rupert Giles, has been expecting her. He's a Watcher, born of the same mystical mythos that brought forth Slayers,

> **FUN FACT:** Selma Blair and Katie Holmes were among the actresses who auditioned for the role of Buffy Summers.

meant to be her guardian and trainer, a spiritual guide. Sunnydale itself is located on a Hellmouth, a portal of demonic energy that attracts all sorts of supernatural wackiness to the area. In other words, it's a town in desperate need of a vampire Slayer. And now, at last, it has one.

Buffy chafes at this knowledge and resists the proverbial call to arms. But when classmates are killed by what can only be vamps, our girl faces up to her calling. In the process, she meets and befriends Willow Rosenberg and Xander Harris, lovable geek best friends who uncover Buffy's identity (to her and Giles's dismay) only to join her in her fight against evil despite the danger.

> "You're the Slayer and we're, like, the Slayerettes!"
>
> —Willow, "Witch"

Through the television show's seven seasons, Buffy faces, as Giles states, "a veritable cornucopia of fiends and devils and ghouls." The highlights— known to loyal viewers colloquially as "Big Bads"—were:

THE MASTER

A centuries-old OG leader of the vamp squad imprisoned beneath the seal of the Hellmouth and determined to open it. He's prophesied to kill the Slayer and, in fact, he does—a little. In point of fact, Buffy drowns after he feeds off her, but she's revived by Xander, proving that even a Slayer gets by with a little help from her friends.

SPIKE AND DRUSILLA
(WITH A SIDE OF ANGEL)

Two punk-rock-Brit-Goth vampires (imagine a more-emo Sid and Nancy) from back in the day with connections to Angel, a vampire with a soul (yes, it's a thing) who also happens to be Buffy's honey and an ally for the cause. The two arrive in Sunnydale with a yen to destroy the Slayer and/or the world, Spike having two prior Slayer kills under his belt. When Angel loses his soul midway through season two and reverts to his evil self, Angelus (yes, it's another thing), he joins them, and Buffy is forced to fight all three.

MAYOR RICHARD WILKINS III

Driving home the notion that Sunnydale higher-ups are aware of the town's demonic population and invested in keeping it on the DL, the Mayor himself is a certified baddie with eyes to "ascend" to full-on demonhood, destroying the school (and eventually the world—are you sensing a theme yet?) on Buffy's graduation day. Long story short, she enlists a willing army of fellow students and blows him up—along with the school. So that's two for two in terms of willful destruction of school property, but at least our girl has a good excuse.

FUN FACT: One of the Mayor's most formidable allies is none other than Faith, a second Slayer (more on that soon) who's gone rogue and seems to be Buffy's utmost foil.

ADAM / THE INITIATIVE

Season four sees Buffy and her friends head off to college (though Xander chooses to opt out, instead getting a job straight out of high school) and, in that process, plunge into the uncertain world of nascent adulthood and newfound independence. At first, Buffy feels insecure about this step but finds her footing (literally) when facing off against a smug group of vamps who've been trawling the campus for fresh meat for some time. But that's before she meets Adam, a demon-machine hybrid created by Buffy's psych professor, of all people (Whedon's got a thing about authority figures, it seems).

Crafted from monster parts collected by the secret government paranormal team, the Initiative (a group to which, Buffy learns, her new crush, the deceptively normal grad student Riley Finn, belongs), Adam is a nod to Frankenstein's monster and a reminder to Buffy that she's strongest when leaning on her friends: her "brain" (Willow) and her "heart" (Xander). Though the intricacies of this new life stage initially destabilize their bond, they come back together to defeat the baddie at the season's end. Afterward, the Initiative disbands and destroys all evidence of their existence. It's all very *X-Files*, as Buffy herself might note.

GLORIFICUS/ "GLORY"

By season five, one might think our Slayer had seen it all—and one would *almost* be right. But Whedon and Co. still manage to surprise viewers and protagonists alike with the introduction of Glory, a snappy, wisecracking blonde (sound familiar?).

She's stronger than any Big Bad Buffy's faced, and after a few extremely painful confrontations, Buffy learns why:

Indeed, Glory is a god from a hell dimension who was cast out by her co-demons after her own thirst for power made her, well . . . a touch difficult to work with. She was banished to Earth and contained in a human vessel: a doctor named Ben, the thinking being that once Ben died, Glory would be gone for good. Glory and Ben alternate physical form, with most humans not realizing or remembering when they've witnessed one transition into the other. In the meantime, she seeks a mystical key: an energy source that will unlock the barrier back to her demon dimension (destroying—say it with me now—all of humanity in the process).

In yet another clever twist, a group of monks sworn to protect the key did so by forging it into human form, resulting in Dawn Summers, Buffy's brand-spanking-new (though not in the gang's modified memories) fifteen-year-old sister. Naturally, Glory's objective is to drain the key—a.k.a. kill Dawn—and naturally, Buffy stops her by sacrificing her own blood to seal the portal that Dawn's blood has opened, dying heroically and fulfilling her mortal Slayer duties in the series' devastating one hundredth episode, "The Gift."

As Buffy has learned, in an earlier prophetic dream, "Death is [her] gift" ("Restless"), and in order to defeat Glory, she gives it freely.

THE TRIO/ DARK WILLOW

Of course, if we've learned anything about Buffy over her first five seasons, it's that not even death keeps a good Slayer down. The Scooby Gang (minus Cordelia, who left the series to star in its spin-off, *Angel*, but joined by Xander and Willow's partners, Anya and Tara, respectively) resurrect Buffy, assuming they're rescuing her from an eternity of languishing in an unknown hell dimension.

Little do they know, they've actually dragged her out of the Buffyverse's equivalent of heaven, and she's shell-shocked, to say the least.

"Wherever I was, I was happy. At peace. I knew that everyone I cared about was all right. I knew it. Time didn't mean anything. Nothing had form. But I was still me, you know? And I was warm. And I was loved. And I was finished. Complete. I don't understand theology, or dimensions, or any of it, really . . . but I think I was in heaven. And now I'm not. I was torn out of there. Pulled out. By my friends. Everything here is hard and bright and violent. Everything I touch, everything I feel. This is hell . . . knowing what I've lost."

—Buffy, "After Life"

She confesses this to a neutered (and therefore allied) Spike, who has fallen in love with Buffy, which makes the revelation all the more devastating. She tells him "they can never know," but when a musical demon comes to town for the infamous musical episode "Once More, with Feeling," she sings her truth, and just about everything comes unraveled.

While season six has an emotionally defeated Slayer struggling with real-world responsibilities (keeping her sister safe, managing their household and finances in the wake of her mother's stubbornly mortal season five death), her foes for this arc are perhaps the most juvenile: "the Trio," a group of geeks from her Sunnydale High days who've teamed up to take over the town.

The Trio consists of Warren Mears, Andrew Wells, and Jonathan Levinson, all of whom are connected to earlier events and prior seasons. While Jonathan and Andrew are peskier than anything, Warren is a true misogynist with evil intentions. Feeling emasculated by the Slayer, he stalks Buffy with a gun, accidentally killing Willow's girlfriend, Tara, in the process.

Willow's use of magic has been growing progressively darker, and the magic "addict" is so consumed by her grief and rage that she magically flays Warren in a fit of revenge. Fueled by dark power, Willow ultimately becomes the Big Bad Buffy must conquer—or risk losing not only the world but one of her dearest friends in the process.

JONATHAN: I still can't believe that was Willow. I mean . . . I've known her almost as long as you guys. Willow was . . . you know. She packed her own lunches and wore floods and she was always . . . just Willow.

[The entire car violently rocks.]

ANDREW: What was that?

XANDER: Just Willow.

—"Two to Go"

For once, though, the Slayer is truly up against a force she can't best. It turns out, the only way to bring back Willow's humanity is through the love and support of Xander, the self-professed "Zeppo" of the group. As introduced in season four, he's the group's "heart" ("Primeval"), and that's reinforced when he's able to get through to Willow.

Buffy doesn't mind sharing the spotlight, though. All's well that ends well enough, and ultimately, evil is defeated and our Slayeretts are closer than ever.

THE FIRST / CALEB

Season seven was the Slayer's swan song, and fittingly, Joss and Co. brought the series full circle: back to Sunnydale High, where Buffy now serves as a guidance counselor of sorts (the lack of formal training doesn't seem to bother anyone, for reasons that later become clear). The school's been rebuilt, and now that it's open for business, our resident superhero wants to keep an eye on things.

Quickly enough, the gang learns that the First evil, a.k.a. a primeval force that's essentially the root of all worldly (and for that matter, otherworldly) badness, is fixing to open the Hellmouth (*déjà vu* much?) and unleash a hoard of primitive vamps unlike anything Buffy has ever faced. Incorporeal by nature, the First can take the form of any person (or creature, in the case of vampires) who's died, giving us encore appearances from old favorites like Joyce. It also seduces an evil preacher, Caleb, into tormenting Buffy at its behest.

It's in season seven that the true feminist promise of Buffy's mythology takes shape. In learning about the depth of her powers, Buffy discovers that the first Slayer was chosen by the original council of Watchers, forcibly imbued with powers (demonic powers, no less) with no regard for consent. Every generation of Slayer to follow thereafter fought—and necessarily died—on behalf of humankind under the Watchers' authority . . . until Buffy, fed up with taking orders, quit answering to the Council and insisted that they work *with* her on *her* terms.

> "You're Watchers. Without a Slayer, you're pretty much just watching *Masterpiece Theater*.... So here's how it's gonna work. You're gonna tell me everything you know. And you're gonna go away."
>
> —Buffy, "Checkpoint"

It turns out, the First had launched a full-scale attack on the Watchers' institution with the goal of taking it all down. The Council headquarters are blown up, and as we've seen throughout early episodes of the season, future Slayers ("Potentials") are targeted and murdered, with the endgame being ridding the world of worthy foes.

"Into every generation, a Slayer is born." ("Welcome to the Hellmouth") *One* girl, we're told (or maybe, at most, two at a time, if the first one happens to have died briefly). But Buffy subverts the Final Girl trope in her bravest, most selfless act as Slayer: she calls on Willow to "activate" every Potential Slayer in the world. She amasses an army that faces off against the First and keeps the world from ending (was there ever any real doubt?). And yes, she does this on behalf of humanity (and, one might argue, for her own sake, too—girl needed a leg up, to be sure). But in activating the Potentials, she literally empowers them in ways many might never have known.

Buffy Summers is a warrior, a Slayer through and through, but more than that, she's a leader. Over the course of the series, she grows into her powers, evolving from foot soldier to general, and eventually giving up her birthright as uniquely Chosen. Though school is never her top priority, she's very bright (her stellar SAT scores in season three take everyone by surprise). Though she's endlessly resilient and willing to make extreme sacrifices (her boyfriend, her own life), she's also warm, caring, and full of love. And when she takes a moment in the last scene of the series finale to contemplate her latest victory, her shared mantle, and her next steps, the smile that crosses her face is entirely hard-won.

WILLOW DANIELLE ROSENBERG

Among diehard *Buffy* fans, there's a subset of viewers who'd put this sidekick
above the eponymous Slayer in their Kickass Ladies of the Whedonverse
rankings. And with good reason: she may have started off as the shy, nerdy
brains behind the Buffster, but over the course of the series, Willow's character
development straight-up exploded.

Willow first encounters Buffy as the Slayer is being given a quickie tour
of Sunnydale High via resident mean girl Cordelia Chase.

CORDELIA: Willow! Nice dress. Good to know you've seen the softer side of Sears.

WILLOW: Uh, oh, well, my mom picked it out.

CORDELIA: No wonder you're such a guy magnet.

—"Welcome to the Hellmouth"

When Buffy asks Willow for homework help later in the episode, Willow balks. She thought Buffy was hanging with Cordelia. ("I can't do both?" "Not legally." "Welcome to the Hellmouth.") Her book smarts come in more than handy, and early episodes feature her helping Giles with research, particularly when his needs are more tech-related. Willow's vulnerability resonated with viewers; by May 1998, seven fan sites had been dedicated to her character. Alyson Hannigan, who played the character in the show, had a theory for the Willow love: "She really is what a lot of high-schoolers are like, with that awkwardness and shyness, and all those adolescent feelings." In other words, Willow is adorable and relatable, even if (or maybe because) she's definitely *not* a "guy magnet."

"When I'm with a boy I like, it's hard for me to say anything cool or witty or at all. I can usually make a few vowel sounds and then I have to go away."

—Willow, "Welcome to the Hellmouth"

In early days, her lingering crush on Xander (they "dated" in kindergarten but broke up when he stole her Barbie) is painfully unrequited. But the sweet, self-deprecating redhead soon catches the eye of cooler-than-thou rocker Daniel "Oz" Osbourne, a quirky, laconic guitarist (who's also secretly "Mr.-Test-Scores!"-genius) ("Dead Man's Party") and who adores Willow at first sight.

As Willow's techno skills evolve, so does her interest in magic, and she's revealed to be an innately powerful witch. Her first forays into spellcasting come in the season two finale, "Becoming, Parts 1 and 2," when she tries to re-ensoul Angel. (She succeeds, but not before Angelus has awakened the demon Acathala, so Buffy still has to kill him and send him to hell. But, hey— points for trying, girl!)

Some efforts are stronger than others, and when she turns fellow classmate (and fellow witch!) Amy into a rat in season three's "Gingerbread," it's a while before she's able to turn her back. ("Maybe we should get her one of those wheel thingees," Buffy suggests.)

It's in college, though, that Willow begins to explore not only her use of magic but also her sexuality. Though she's frustrated with her UC Sunnydale campus's underwhelming Wicca group ("buncha wanna blessed-be's") ("Hush"), it's there she meets Tara Maclay, another shy, sweet student with latent magical powers. In season four's "Hush," the girls grab hands in an effort to ward off the Gentlemen, and only together does their power move objects and keep them safe.

(It's a pretty solid metaphor.)

The two quickly become inseparable, and Tara and Willow just as quickly establish themselves as one of the most progressive onscreen couples in television history. As *Nerdist* wrote in 2017, "*Buffy the Vampire Slayer* was one of the first TV shows to depict a naturally progressing relationship between two women that wasn't for ratings and wasn't a punchline. For many young viewers, this was the first time they had ever seen gay characters fall in love and find acceptance among their peers."

Not that network television was fully ready for it. Initially, Willow and Tara were mostly seen casting spells behind closed doors while other couples were getting more directly down and dirty. (Specifically, an entire episode of season four is dedicated to ghosts summoned by the force of Buffy and Riley's sexual chemistry.) In "Who Are You," the Wiccans' magic leaves them sweaty and breathless—Whedon was

working to make a point while still skirting censorship.

Willow and Tara's first on-screen kiss happens in season five's "The Body," as the two are preparing—with great emotional pain and turmoil—to attend Joyce Summers's funeral. Nonetheless, all along the way, Whedon stayed true to his promise to fans that he would not "promote the hell out of a same-sex relationship for exploitation value that [we] take back by the end of the [episode]."

This being Joss Whedon's world, of course, no romantic couple is allowed to stay happy for *too* long (love is pain in the Buffyverse, if you hadn't noticed). Slowly, Willow's powers grow, and with them grows her hunger for power itself. Willow's abuse of magic becomes an addiction—she's a magic junkie, it turns out, which is every bit as dangerous as a *junkie* junkie—and her illness leads her to become the Big Bad of season six. Among other major consequences, Tara leaves her when it becomes clear Willow can't quit. (As discussed, Tara's death at the hands of Warren is also a big factor in Willow's fall.)

Season seven sees Willow nervously working to navigate the world of witchcraft in a responsible way. We learn that she's spent a summer training with colleagues of Giles's in England, and though she's hesitant and humbled, back with her friends, she's also reconnected to her innate humanity, that quality that spawned so many fan sites in the first place. When Buffy gathers a group of Potential Slayers in her home to train and protect them against the First, Willow and a Potential named Kennedy fall in love, eventually leading to the first lesbian sex scene on broadcast television.

And when Willow casts a spell to imbue all the Potentials with their full Slayer power in the series finale? She's terrified that the process will bring back "Dark Willow," but she's the only one stronger than the men who created Slayers in the first place. And when she does give herself over to the magic completely, her hair goes sheer, stark white with good-magic vibes. It's a potent capper for a character who's journeyed a true redemption arc, and it speaks volumes about what literal "girl power" means on *Buffy*—which is to say, it's everything.

There's a reason "just" Willow is so (justly) beloved, after all.

FUN FACT: **Sarah Michelle Gellar and Alyson Hannigan are the only two stars from the show to appear in all of its 144 episodes.**

CORDELIA CHASE

And speaking of character redemptions . . . this brings us to queen bee (or, as her vanity plate reads, QUEEN C) Cordelia. Initially, she's Buffy's first "friend" at Sunnydale High, impressed by Buffy's valley-girl vibe and cool L.A. cred. ("I'd kill to live in L.A.," she says, in "Welcome to the Hellmouth." "That close to that many shoes.") After a quick pop-culture quiz, Cordelia approves Buffy for socializing only to ditch her when she befriends nerds Xander and Willow.

(Willow was right about the social laws of high school, it turns out.)

At first, Cordelia serves mainly as a foil for Buffy and friends—and a contrast for the blissfully vapid life Buffy's left behind—often needing rescue from Buffy despite her ongoing disdain for the Scooby Gang. But Cordelia's focus on social standing in some ways belies her inherently practical approach to life, which is another trademark of Cordy's. The girl is strong, unwavering, and sturdy: she knows what she wants, and she gets it, whether it's a pair of shoes or Buffy as her double date to a frat party that she *needs* to attend.

Initially, Cordelia seems to have eyes on Angel (she's stunned and skeptical when Buffy tells her he's a vampire), but it's not until she (reluctantly) falls for Xander—against their better judgment—that we start to see the real nuances to her character. Hiding from a demon assassin in Buffy's basement, she and Xander bicker incessantly until the only thing left to do is kiss. Though she tries to break it off with him (after some pressure from her friends), by the end of "Bewitched, Bothered, and Bewildered," Cordy's come to her senses. She acknowledges her feelings for Xander and lays some serious truth on her so-called friends:

"Do you know what you are, Harmony? You're a sheep. . . . All you ever do is what everyone else does just so you can say you did it first. And here I am, scrambling for your approval, when I'm way cooler than you are 'cause I'm not a sheep. I do what I wanna do, and I wear what I wanna wear. And you know what? I'll date whoever the hell I wanna date. No matter *how* lame he is!"

—Cordelia, "Bewitched, Bothered, and Bewildered"

Cordelia's snobbery is grounded in an almost ruthless pragmatism to the point where she's able to outsmart vampires with only her tough talk ("Homecoming"), and when Buffy becomes briefly telepathic in season three's "Earshot," Cordelia's inner thoughts are the only ones that directly mirror the words that she speaks. ("Tact is just not saying true stuff," she says in "Killed by Death." "I'll pass.") She's reliable and loyal, even when she'd rather be doing anything but helping out the Scooby Gang. Like Buffy, her SAT scores reveal an unexpected intellect ("I can't have layers?" she asks in "Choices"), but her wits are generally applied to bending the world to her will.

In fact, one of the few times she can't have her own way is when Xander cheats on her (a "clothes fluke" with him and Willow when they're trying on outfits for the school formal leads to new feelings between the old friends). Her complete devastation at learning of his infidelity is strong enough to summon a vengeance demon to Sunnydale, and in the process, she briefly conjures a bizarre alternate-universe Sunnydale in which Xander and Willow are vampires.

(Worth mentioning: Even in this alternate reality, they're still together. And together, they kill Cordy.)

This being the Buffyverse, status quo is reinstated (though the vengeance demon, Anyanka "Anya" Jenkins remains in town, having been stripped of her powers and forced to attend high school like a regular mortal teen). As season three progresses, Cordelia mostly tries to stay out of the Scoobies' path. In

"The Prom," Xander discovers that, thanks to an "eensy mistake" on their tax returns, Cordelia's family has lost all of their money, and she's working as a sales clerk at a local boutique to make enough money to keep up the façade of her former life.

"I'm a nametag girl now," she tells him through clenched teeth, working to buy a prom dress on layaway. Xander buys her the dress as a surprise, leading to a détente between the two. Of course, she stuns at the prom.

Cordelia's tenure on *Buffy* was cut short, though. After graduation day, when she helps her fellow classmates defeat the Mayor-turned-snake-demon (. . .yeah), she leaves for L.A. to pursue an acting career. Her story continues on the spin-off, *Angel*, which premiered back-to-back with *Buffy*'s fourth season, following Angel's move to the City of Angels to "help the helpless."

It's Cordelia who applies her sunny determination to Angel Investigations, professionalizing the small operation and eventually even generating an income for their team. Cordy's character continues to evolve, and she eventually develops superhuman powers of her own. But to original-flavor *Buffy* fans, she'll always be the bitchy cheerleader—with layers!—that viewers (like Buffy and her friends themselves) truly love to hate.

"You think I'm never lonely just 'cause I'm so cute and popular? I can be surrounded by people and be completely alone. It's not like any of them really know me. I don't even know if they really *like* me half the time. Sometimes when I talk, everyone's so busy agreeing with me, they don't hear a word I say."

—Cordelia, "Out of Sight, Out of Mind"

Don't worry, Cordy. We hear you loud and clear, and we're here for it.

FAITH LEHANE

> "Want. Take. Have."
>
> —Faith, "Bad Girls"

If Kendra, the Vampire Slayer—the first "second Slayer" to arrive on-scene—was Buffy's by-the-book foil, then Faith Lehane is her bizarro self. In the dichotomy of light and dark, good and evil, dutiful and impulsive, and even, heartbreakingly, supported and alone (also easy to read as privileged and not), Faith is quickly shorthanded as "the bad Slayer." She's salty, sassy, and drowning in heavy eyeliner—code for "slutty" in Whedon's world of easy-listening feminism. We could argue that, in this context, poor, faithless Faith never really had a chance of true heroism. But we love her just the same.

Faith shows up in Sunnydale early in season three, just as Buffy is coming to terms with having killed Angel *after* his soul was restored.

The newcomer plays at carefree bad girl, getting her dance on with a vamp at the Bronze then luring him outside for some high-energy stake-age. Buffy, for her part, stands by watching. ("Couldn'ta done it without you," Faith quips, after grabbing Buffy's stake to dispatch of the vampire.)

While the Scoobies are delighted by the cheeky newcomer (Xander, in particular, is captivated by her tales of co-ed naked Slaying), Buffy quickly feels judged and threatened. Faith tells her (and her friends seem to agree) she needs to loosen up, to "find the fun."

Buffy complains to Giles that she's feeling "single white femaled" by her "zesty" new Slayer; but it turns out, it's more complicated than that.

Faith *said* she'd come to Sunnydale to compare notes with the infamous Buffy while her Watcher was away. But actually, her Watcher is dead, killed by an uber-vamp named

Kakistos (Greek for "worst of the worst"). And now Kakistos is after Faith. Though the two mismatched Slayers are at odds when he shows up on Faith's doorstep, they quickly fall into lockstep despite their different fighting styles and do away with him. Giles arranges for temporary custody of Faith and voilà, double the Slayers, double the fun.

For a time, at least. Buffy realizes there's an upside to having a partner in this dangerous calling, but Faith's hedonistic, impulsive approach to their vocation has its negatives. She's all stake first, ask questions later. As a method, it's not without its risks.

In "Bad Girls," Faith briefly lures Buffy over to the darker side of Slaying—some sexy dancing at the Bronze followed by a deliriously gleeful staking romp across town. They steal weapons and evade the police. But in the heat of their rampage, Faith accidentally stakes a human. Buffy is devastated (and her more puritanical approach to Slaying is obviously validated). Faith is visibly shaken but hides behind her tough-girl persona, insisting it doesn't matter. Here, the cornerstone of her personality—instability, vulnerability, and bravado—are established; and as viewers, we ache for her even as she's willfully self-destructing.

As science fiction author A. M. Dellamonica says,

"I don't usually feel all that much sympathy for fictional characters who are throwing gas on their own infernos of self-destruction, but Eliza Dushku as Faith has me every step of the way in this episode. The gulf between that girl who's scrubbing the blood out of her clothes in the crappy hotel and the polished way she pretends to be okay with it all is vast and sad. Dushku might have been born to play this particular lost girl as she swan-dives to her doom."

Buffy, of course, wants to come clean, but Faith isn't having it. Her quest to cover up the truth eventually leads to her full-on corruption, as she's recruited by the Mayor as a femme-Nikita/girl Friday hybrid and double agent while he counts down toward his Ascension. Even in her betrayal of our heroine, it's easy to see why Faith makes the choices she does: she has no family, her Watcher died, and she's been used and discarded by most of the people she's known. She was built for killing and given powers she can barely cope with, and those who should be working with her to put those powers to use seem to spend an awful lot of time criticizing her methods not to mention her sanity. For Faith, the Mayor's approval—and obvious admiration of her own Slayer skills and physical prowess—is paramount, irresistible. "No Slayer of mine is going to live in a fleabag motel," he tells her, and moves her into

a beautiful apartment, showering her in new clothes, gifts, and everything she might need to defeat Buffy and Co. But she *doesn't* defeat them, and at the end of season three, she's in a plot-convenient coma, taking her offscreen for a while. She reappears in season four with a little party favor from the now-deceased Mayor: a charm that allows her to swap bodies with Buffy.

Faith-as-Buffy has all sorts of fun and wreaks all sorts of havoc while basking in the glow of being the *good* Chosen One, for once. Her first plan is to skip town in Buffy's body and leave "Faith" to deal with the consequences. (Legal issues aside, the Watchers' Council is all out of patience with Faith, it seems.) But she can't resist seducing Buffy's boyfriend, Riley, and messing with her friends and family. Playing Buffy is a head trip, though, and soon enough she's jumped to fight some vampires who've taken over a church. When Buffy shows up to get her body back, Faith straight-up *unleashes* on her, the depths of her self-hatred brutally evident as she pummels her own body.

Back in her own skin, Faith is taken by the Watchers' Council. "I guess she's had her fun," Buffy's Riley says, as they rehash. "Yeah . . . fun . . ." Buffy says. Having spent time in Faith's literal body, she has a new perspective on just how deep the girl's self-loathing is. It's a perspective that comes in handy in season seven, when Faith escapes prison and heads to Sunnydale to fight the First alongside Buffy and the Potentials.

(True to form, she's understandably hurt that Buffy didn't think to protect *her* from the Bringers, who were systematically taking out anyone with Slayer lineage, not to mention even *warn* her of what was going on. "Something's killing girls all over the world, trying to end the Slayer line," she says in "Dirty Girls."

"Thing like that, figure I might get a heads-up."

("Faith—we didn't think—" Willow protests. But also true to form, Faith shrugs her off. "I get by," she says.)

When Faith finds Buffy, she's surprised to discover Buffy fighting alongside Spike (who also has a soul now. It's the hot new accessory for fall, haven't you heard?). "You protecting vampires? Are you the bad Slayer now? Am I the good Slayer now?"

It's . . . complicated, and, like most characters (especially the empowered women) on *Buffy*, good and evil aren't always cut-and-dried. For a minute, it even looks like there might be a coup, when the Potentials elect Faith (against her will, but still . . .) to be their leader over Buffy, ousting Buffy from her own home. But Faith is given her hero's moment in the finale arc, kicking ass in the final (televised) apocalypse and even being rewarded with a love interest in the form of grade-A hottie Principal Wood.

It's like the saying goes: you gotta have Faith.

ANYANKA "ANYA" CHRISTINA EMANUELLA JENKINS

For a show that gives so much lip service (and screen time!) to girl power, it must be said: very few baddies on *Buffy* hath the fury of a woman scorned. Heartbreak is one of the strongest catalysts for conflict on the series (think Angel

and Buffy, Spike and Dru, Oz and Willow . . . just for starters). As Buffy herself says, "Love makes you do the wacky." And Anya knows that better than anyone.

A one-time vengeance demon with a "thing" about jilted women, Anya is called to Sunnydale in season three by the force of Cordelia's pain. After Cordy learns that Xander's been cheating on her with Willow, her humiliation is practically palpable.

Anya was originally a human named Aud, but she spent over a thousand years as Anyanka, a vengeance demon who grants wishes to wronged women. She appears in "The Wish," fulfilling Cordelia's passion-fueled request: that Buffy Summers had never shown her face in Sunnydale.

ANYA: Xander, he's an utter loser. Don't you wish…

CORDELIA: I never would've looked at Xander twice if Buffy hadn't made him marginally cooler by hanging with him… I wish Buffy Summers had never come to Sunnydale.

ANYA (AS ANYANKA): Done.

—"The Wish"

Alas, Cordy really hasn't given thought to the full ramifications of this wish. ("She was like a good fairy . . . A scary, veiny good fairy.")

To be clear: Anya is no good fairy. And this version of Sunnydale is no fairy tale. In this alternate reality, Sunnydale's been completely overtaken by vamps: the town has a curfew and students dress in drab, muted colors less likely to attract vampires. Regular memorials are held for those killed by vamps. A puzzled Harmony updates Cordelia: of course, Xander Harris is but a blip

on the radar; he's dead. When Buffy does show up (she's been Slaying in Cleveland), she's killed by the Master with ruthless efficiency. Luckily, Giles destroys Anyanka's pendant, demolishing her power source and reversing the curse. Anya is rendered mortal again.

ANYA: For a thousand years, I wielded the power of the wish. I brought ruin upon the heads of unfaithful men. I offered destruction and chaos for the pleasure of lower beings. I was feared and worshipped across the mortal globe, and now I'm stuck at Sunnydale High! A mortal! A child! And I'm flunking math.

D'HOFFRYN: This is no concern of ours. You will live out your mortal life and die.

—"Doppelgangland"

Stuck in human form, Anya does her best to acclimate. She develops an unlikely crush on Xander, and though she's pathologically blunt and excruciatingly socially awkward, she eventually wins him over with sheer persistence.

ΛΠΥΛ: You can laugh, but I have witnessed a millennium of treachery and oppression from the males of the species. I have nothing but contempt for the whole libidinous lot of them.

ΧΛΠDER: Then why are you talking to me?

ΛΠΥΛ: I don't have a date for the prom.

ΧΛΠDER: Gosh, I wonder why not. Couldn't possibly have anything to do with your sales pitch.

ΛΠΥΛ: [testily] Men are evil. [vulnerably] Will you go with me?

ΧΛΠDER: One of us is very confused, and I honestly don't know which.

—"The Prom"

Despite the improbability of their relationship, Anya and Xander continue to date, and in season five, they get engaged as they're preparing to fight Glory.

However, after thousands of years as a demon, Anya has completely lost touch with any interpersonal skills she may have once had; she's tactless and indiscrete, often annoying people and embarrassing Xander. (She's also inexplicably terrified of bunnies.) She's unabashedly capitalist and values money way more than friendships with other people. Her experiential knowledge does come in handy, though, as she tends to have the inside scoop on some of the evil that the gang encounters. She eventually takes over the local Magic Shop and is accepted as one of the Scoobies. But a demon seeking revenge scares Xander from going through with their marriage hours before they're set to

walk down the aisle, and Anya herself is abandoned like so many of the women for whom she's enacted revenge.

Her former demon boss, D'Hoffryn, learns of her grief and offers her the chance to become a demon again. She accepts, even though her time as a human has rendered her a bit of a softy, and she gains a reputation for granting half-hearted vengeance wishes.

As a demon (again), it's only a matter of time before Anya is up against Buffy; the battle goes poorly for her (to say the least), Anya is shamed, and once it's done, she's been stripped of her powers yet again. In "Selfless," the series explores Anya's lack of personal identity, and at the episode's end, she tells Xander she needs to find her purpose. Her purpose eventually leads her to team up with Buffy and gang yet again to fight the First. She's killed swiftly and without fanfare in the series finale, without any of her friends even given the chance to confirm that she's fallen. Whether she deserved better is a question. Certainly, she's one of the more morally ambiguous babes of Buffy. But she was funny and forthright, and to be fair, from what we see of her backstory, she never did have much of a chance at being "normal." The world never was very "good" to her. She usually came through when it mattered.

In the canon of Buffy and a world of men seeking to dominate, violate, and betray the women who love them, having a spunky, strong voice that is literally looking to even the score and advocate on women's behalf is pretty damn magical.

"I guess I just realized how amazingly . . . screwed up [people] are. I mean really, really screwed up in a monumental fashion. And they have no purpose that unites them, so they just drift around, blundering through life until they die. Which they know is coming, and yet every single one of them is surprised when it happens to them. They're incapable of thinking about what they want beyond the moment. They kill each other, which is clearly insane. And yet, here's the thing:

When it's something that really matters, they fight. I mean, they're lame morons for fighting, but they do. They never . . . they never quit. And so I guess I will keep fighting, too."

—Anya, "End of Days"

TARA MACLAY

When Willow-Willow meets Vamp-Willow in season three's "Doppelgangland," her first impression of her alter ego boils down to "I'm so evil and skanky. And I think I'm kinda gay." Her demon doppelganger certainly seems to have a more open, curious attitude toward sexuality than the shy, insecure human who was catfished by an internet demon in season one. It feels like a throwaway line in the moment, but when Tara Maclay arrives on the scene in season four, an otherwise casual comment gets upgraded to something much more prophetic.

Tara meets Willow for the first time at the UC Sunnydale's Wiccan group meeting. Willow has complained to Buffy that none of the women in the group are actual witches, but it turns out that Tara has real powers that she's interested in learning to use and grow, just like Willow.

The two girls find themselves alone on campus one night, pursued by the Gentlemen, terrifying creatures who render their victims mute. The girls hide in a classroom and attempt to barricade the door telekinetically but can't until, instinctively, they join hands. Together, their power intensifies exponentially, and they succeed. Magic.

Tara is shy and soft-spoken (with an occasional stutter that gets worse when she's nervous), but she's eager to get to know Willow. Their relationship remains platonic for a little while, as their exploration of magic becomes a metaphor for their exploration of their sexual feelings for each other. When Oz, who abruptly left Willow earlier in the season to try to tame his werewolf instincts, returns, he immediately senses the intimacy between the girls. (In fact, it causes him to wolf out and attack Tara, which isn't excellent for anyone involved. But in the end, it's okay.)

When Willow comes to see Tara after she's bid Oz a final farewell, Tara tells her, "You have to be with the person you love." To which Willow replies, "I am."

For a while, the two are happily ensconced in a love bubble, but Tara meets the rest of the Scoobies when Faith comes to town to bodysnatch Buffy. It's actually Tara who realizes Faith has hijacked Buffy's body, which is, it must be said, a fairly kick-ass first impression to make on one's significant other's friends.

> "A person's energy has a flow, a unity. Buffy's was fragmented; it grated, like something forced in where it doesn't belong. Plus she was kind of mean."
>
> —Tara, "Who Are You"

In season five, Tara is attacked by Glory, who sucks the energy from her to replenish herself on Earth (as she's known to do). It's a process that leaves Tara—and all of Glory's brain-sucked victims—completely insane. Though her mind is eventually restored, in season six, Willow casts a spell to wipe Tara's memory so that Tara will forget a fight the two have been having. Tara's hurt that Willow would (literally) mess with her head after what she'd gone through with Glory, but she's also concerned that Willow's been using too much magic (and she's not the only one, but she's the most vocal—and the one whose opinion matters perhaps

the most). She challenges Willow to go a day without using any magic.

Willow fails the challenge—massively—and attempts to cover up her use of magic with a spell to augment the gang's memory, which is not only a violation of the promise she made to Tara but a violation of her loved ones' *minds*. Tara is absolutely crushed, and she leaves Willow in one of the most devastating (despite also being, at times, downright hilarious) episodes of all time, "Tabula Rasa."

Tara manages to stay away even as Willow continues to spiral out of control, but she does have contact with the rest of the Scoobies here and there. Her soft-spoken, nonjudgmental demeanor means that she's actually the one Buffy confides in about the fact that she's been sleeping with Spike (. . . that's a whole 'nother thing). Eventually, Tara comes back to give Willow another chance, and the two are given exactly one night together in reconciled bliss . . . before a stray bullet from Warren kills Tara and sends Willow over the edge.

Season six saw *Buffy* move networks to UPN, and with it, the show took a decidedly dark turn. (Opening on Buffy being resurrected from her grave was a bold move and set the tone, it turned out.) It's a notoriously divisive season among fans, some of whom argue that the show strayed too far from its original conception and that characters' choices had gone from being self-destructive to straight-up out of character.

Specifically, Tara's death left many reeling not only for the pathos it stirred up, but also for the fact that one of network television's first openly gay characters had to be killed off and that, subsequently, Willow's arc fell into the "evil lesbian" trope.

For a show that had offered so subversive—and hopeful!—a model, killing Tara felt cheap. Never mind that the show was notorious for killing off important characters (Ms. Calendar, Joyce); the Willow-Tara 'ship had become iconic for a million good reasons, and the choice to kill Tara and punish Willow was loaded.

Marti Noxon, one of the series' showrunners, has said in interviews that she regrets killing off Tara. Like fans, she's willing to concede that season six storylines bordered on "sadistic."

In a post on *The Mary Sue*, a blogger notes,

"My issue with Willow and Tara was their legacy as *the* benchmark queer relationship in genre television that all female queer couples are matched up against. Tara being shot . . . was a 'bury your gays' moment that has rightfully lived in infamy ever since. Especially because of the repercussions of the death for Willow as a character."

One of the primary criticisms lobbed at *Buffy* through the lens of our modern landscape is its lack of inclusivity, and that argument certainly extends to the lack of LGBTQ representation. But that doesn't take away from the ground-breaking moments that Willow and Tara had on-screen that paved the way for a more progressive pop-culture-verse. Willow and Tara were a flawed couple, for sure, but as a main character on a network television show, Tara Maclay was ahead of her time.

TARA: Every time I . . . even at my worst, you always make me feel special. How do you do that?

WILLOW: Magic.

—"Family"

HONORARY MENTIONS

There's a strong argument to be made for the previous entries as the definitive First Ladies of the Buffdom. But fans know that's hardly where the girl power ends in the Slayerverse. As such, we've compiled a primer of the best of the rest—secondary, perhaps, but still integral to the messages that *Buffy* sent about strong women and their (vital) place in our world. They're presented here in order of series appearance.

DARLA

Darla is notable for having a big impact in very few episodes. We see her first in the series pilot, an acolyte of the Master. Her first line is the very first line of the series: "Are you sure this is a good idea?"

She's presented to us as the classic helpless blonde of a thousand slasher movies, the ones *Bitch* knew we'd be trying to warn. But, as soon as the boy assures her that there's no one around, that it's "safe" (and, of course, the viewer knows it's not, though at this point we're still not expecting the twist), she turns and *morphs* into a vicious vampire, immediately attacking her companion.

It's sharp and visceral, and the moment announced to viewers that this show was not going to follow the classic tropes of a thousand slasher movies before it. The women in this show are the ones with the real power, and we underestimate them at our own peril.

Darla is the vampire who sired Angel, and the two were linked for generations on a path of destruction. She can't help but be a little jealous of his feelings for Buffy. Yes, it's a cliché, and it's one of the rare moments where the

show fails the Bechdel test miserably. Darla attacks Joyce in an effort to frame Angel and turn Buffy against him. Her ruse fails, and while she's stalking Buffy, Angel kills her. Her last words are " . . . Angel?" just before she turns to dust ("Angel").

It'd be easier to argue her feminist qualities if her storyline on *Buffy* weren't so intrinsically linked to a man (er, a male vamp, in any case). And actress Julie Benz has admitted in interviews that her instinct was to play Darla "like the jilted ex-wife."

Though her stint on *Buffy* is short-lived, like Cordelia and Faith, she goes on to have an extended role on *Angel*, where we get a little more insight into her backstory. (She was a prostitute dying of syphilis when she was turned.) Darla is evil, but she's straightforward and, in her own twisted way, pure. And her love for Angel feels almost human.

Almost.

JOYCE SUMMERS

One of the few Buffy babes who doesn't have any sort of paranormal power or secret identity (even Cordelia gets visions once she relocates to L.A. and joins forces with Angel), Joyce is nonetheless essential to our understanding of Buffy herself. (Chalk it up to the whole being-her-mother thing.)

She's Buffy's first female role model, primary caretaker, and primary family relationship. It's established in the pilot that Buffy and her mother are on their own since her parents' (somewhat recent) divorce. Joss Whedon is notoriously rough on dads in his work, and *Buffy* is no exception. While Buffy's father makes a few appearances in early episodes, he's depicted as largely checked out and gradually fades from the picture.

At first glance, Joyce is given little more than "harried single mom" status, struggling to cope with a problem child who, among other things, burns down school gymnasiums. In one of the first

scenes of the pilot, she drops Buffy off for her first day at Sunnydale High with a cheery "Try not to get kicked out!"

Early episodes focus mainly on the protracted "high school is hell" metaphor and Buffy's struggle to balance her calling with normal teenage girlhood. As such, Joyce's role is relegated to (somewhat willfully) ignorant parent, an obstacle to Buffy's secret identity, and the ultimate parent who "just doesn't get it" (because who could?).

In season two, Buffy "comes out" to her mother as the Slayer, and initially, Joyce's reaction isn't the best. She first refuses to believe what Buffy's telling her and then orders Buffy to stay home (and not go out to fight Angel and stop Acathala). When Buffy storms past her, Joyce tells her, "If you walk out that door, don't even think of coming back."

Accordingly, once the battle is over, Buffy skips town. When she comes back in season three, Joyce welcomes her but admits, in the heat of an argument, that she's furious with Buffy for leaving in the first place.

BUFFY: But you told me! You're the one who said I should go. You said—if you leave this house, don't come back. You found out who I really am and you couldn't deal—remember?

JOYCE: You didn't give me any time! You just dumped this thing on me and expected me to get it. . . . Well guess what, Mom's not perfect. . . . But that doesn't give you the right to punish me by running away.

—"Dead Man's Party"

Aware of Buffy's birthright as Slayer, though, as of season three, Joyce is admirably adept at balancing support and understanding with concern and also a hope for Buffy to someday have a future beyond just slaying. Their mother-daughter relationship is healthy and close and deepens with the arrival of Dawn, Buffy's retconned younger sister.

Being a single woman living on a Hellmouth, Joyce's love life is accordingly doomed. One of her early suitors turns out to be a homicidal robot, and some cursed candy leads her to an ill-advised romp with Giles that neither ever completely lives down. In season five, she has a promising date with a new prospect, but unfortunately she dies in the stellar, somber episode "The Body" due to complications from a brain tumor surgery. Buffy struggles to fill the hole left behind, and this excruciating rite of passage into adulthood is just one of the real-world challenges on the Slayer's plate.

Joyce, you were a strong woman and a supportive, caring mother. You are missed.

HARMONY KENDALL

Yet another "dumb blonde" from the annals of *Buffy*, we first meet Harmony in her role as a Cordette—she's flanking Cordelia when Buffy first meets Queen C in the pilot. While she's presented as one of Cordy's underlings, she does hold some power; Cordelia breaks up with Xander (briefly) in season two because Harmony (speaking on behalf of their clique) writes him off as a dork. She's chastened when Cordelia pushes back, and their friendship seems to stay (mostly) steady through "Graduation Day," when Harmony, too, is recruited to fight against the Mayor.

(It's worth mentioning that when Xander cheats on Cordelia, Harmony is downright *evil* about it, feigning sympathy when in fact her end game—at which she succeeds—is to make Cordelia feel even worse.)

But as we know, Joss Whedon is all about the twists, and the next time we see Harmony, it's season four, Buffy's in college, and Harmony, too, has gone through some . . . changes. Sure, she's still vapid, shallow, and looks-obsessed (she also has a thing for unicorns, it turns out), but she's also a vampire. And she's dating *Spike*.

> "Harmony? A vampire? She must be dying without a reflection."
>
> —Buffy, "The Harsh Light of the Day"

How Harmony and Spike first got together is anyone's guess—one has to assume Spike was feeling a little desperate after Drusilla left him, humiliatingly, for a fungus demon—and Spike treats Harmony with complete contempt. She acknowledges that he doesn't respect her, but the two have a strong sexual attraction, and she stays even beyond her better judgment.

"I don't know why I let you be so mean to me," she whines in "The Harsh Light of the Day." Spike simply says, "Love hurts, baby."

Their relationship goes beyond being twisted to being straight up abusive when Spike stakes her to silence her prattle. Thanks to a magic gem, she survives, and it's the push she needs to finally leave him. (Unfortunately, it's only the first step in what's to be a long, somewhat redundant process.)

Becoming a vampire doesn't miraculously transform Harmony, but at least she eventually manages to stand up for herself a little. Maybe we could all take a cue from Harmony and access our more "monstrous" (a.k.a. less "girlie") side and be agents of our own relationships?

JENNY CALENDAR /
JANNA OF THE KALDERASH

Jenny Calendar is the computer teacher at Sunnydale High. Hip, modern, and pretty, she immediately stands out as one of the "cooler" adults on the faculty. We meet her in season one's "I Robot, You Jane," after a project to scan books into the school's library system results in a demon being unleashed into the internet. Giles is appalled to see technology encroach on his sacred space, and Jenny teases him mercilessly for his outdated attitudes.

"I know our ways are strange to you, but soon you will join us in the twentieth century . . . with three whole years to spare!"

—Jenny, "I Robot, You Jane"

As soon as the demon is identified, Giles realizes he's not equipped to exorcise it from the web without an IT assist. He's worried about how to break the news to Jenny, but she makes it easy when she cuts him off with a simple "There's a demon on the internet." It turns out, she's a "technopagan," familiar with spellcasting and magic. She helps the Scoobies defeat the demon and goes on to become Giles's love interest. (Opposites do attract, after all!)

All seems well for our resident oldsters (give or take a demonic possession or two) until season two, when Buffy and Angel's relationship heats up. Fans know that after they have sex, Angel's gypsy curse is broken and he loses his soul. Turns out, "Jenny Calendar" is actually "Janna" of the Kalderash clan, a gypsy from the very clan that cursed Angel once upon a time. It's no secret that she's in Sunnydale; she

was sent there to keep tabs on Angel and to be sure he "still suffers" ("Surprise").

When the gang finds out that Jenny's been hiding her true identity, they're understandably devasted. A contrite Jenny tries to decipher the spell to curse Angel again; but in his evil form, Angelus finds her, destroys her work (or so it seems), and kills her, leaving her laid out on Giles's bed in a tragic, grisly tableau.

Death being less of an issue on *Buffy* than on other shows, she does come back in various hallucinated states, including tormenting Angel during an existential crisis in season three. Of all the various deaths Buffy is unable to prevent, Ms. Calendar's seems to hit her the hardest. We know just how she feels. On *Buffy*, being an evolved, independent woman doesn't automatically preclude suffering. Funny—we could say the same about real life, too.

DRUSILLA

One half of the devious duo of Spike and Dru, Drusilla is the Nancy to Spike's Sid, a frail, insane, Gothic bloom of a character who walks the fine line of absurdity and threat with precision and grace. Her physical appearance—lithe, pale, lilting—is said to have been drawn from Kate Moss and the nineties' heroin chic aesthetic.

ANGEL: I did a lot of unconscionable things when I was a vampire. Drusilla was the worst. She was . . . an obsession of mine. She was pure, and sweet, and chaste.

BUFFY: And you made her a vampire.

ANGEL: First I made her insane. Killed everybody she loved. Visited every mental torture on her I could devise. She eventually fled to a convent, and on the day she took her holy orders, I turned her into a demon.

—"Lie to Me"

Giles tells Buffy that Dru was reportedly killed by an angry mob in Prague, but Buffy tells him, "They don't make angry mobs like they used to," because lo and behold, she's in town. At first, Drusilla is still weak and recovering, making her vulnerable and therefore a useful bartering chip for Buffy. But after a ritual to restore her strength that results in a battle royale with Buffy, she's back to full-power badness, while Spike is relegated to a wheelchair. When evil Angelus seeks out the two, she's eager for the old friends to be back together again— and her relationship with Angel is definitely not strictly platonic.

After striking a deal with Buffy to double-cross Angel in the season

two finale, Spike cuts out of town with an unconscious Dru at his side. We learn in season three that she left him after that, telling him he'd gone soft for having colluded with the Slayer. She pops up again in L.A. on *Angel*, ready to re-sire her vamp-mama Darla (who is now human and dying of syphilis, as she'd been when she was originally mortal). She returns to Sunnydale in season five's "Crush," wanting to persuade Spike to come back to the "family" fold. But by then, Spike has fully fallen for Buffy and offers to stake Drusilla to prove it to her. The course of true love never did run smoothly, and if one thing is clear on *Buffy*, it's that toxic relationships put us at great personal risk.

DAWN SUMMERS

Poor Dawn. It must be rough enough, having a wicked-powerful vampire Slayer as an older sister. (The sibling rivalry in a Slayer's family? That's gotta be *killer*.) But when you accidentally discover that you're not even human but really a swirling mass of mystical energy that a bunch of monks fashioned into human form? That you were sent, in human form, to the Slayer as a sister, complete with a set of implanted memories for the whole crew so that no one will be the wiser to the ruse? But then the truth comes out, everyone's shocked and weirded out, and also the evil god who's after you is, well, *after you* and literally hell-bent on destroying you so she can escape her earthly prison?

Yeah, that's gotta be kind of a head trip. No wonder Dawn is always such a crank.

Another love-to-hate entry in the later seasons of *Buffy*, Dawn elicits strong responses from fans. (She was listed in *TV Guide*'s "The Most Loathed TV Characters of All Time," for one.) She's needy, she's whiny, she's a prime example of that last-ditch "introduce a new character when the story's starting to age," Cousin-Oliver effect. Whedon's plan was to drop her straight into season five with minimal backstory or explanation, and so he did. At the very end of season five, episode one, Buffy comes into her bedroom to find Dawn there. "What are you doing in here?" It's a fake-out, of course, as the viewer assumes Dawn is as much a stranger to Buffy as she is to us. But then off-screen, we hear from Joyce: "Buffy, if you're going out, why don't you take your sister?" To which Dawn and Buffy both protest in unison, "MOM!"

And, scene.

The following episode, "Real Me," follows Dawn's perspective as she endures a day in the life of the Slayer's kid sister. We open with her writing in her diary:

"Nobody knows who I am. Not the real me. It's like nobody cares enough to find out. I mean, does anyone ever ask me what I want to do with my life? Or what my opinion is on stuff? Or what restaurant to order from? No!!! ... No one understands. No one has an older sister who's the Slayer. ... I could so save the world if somebody handed me superpowers. But I'd think of a cool name and wear a mask to protect my loved ones, which Buffy doesn't even."

Over the course of the episode, we get Dawn's take on the Scoobies, Riley (Buffy's boyfriend-du-jour), and general life in Sunnydale (among other things, she has a crush on Xander).

Dawn's inner monologue is cleverly obscure, straddling the line between typical emo-tween prattle and legitimate paranormal threat. At the end of the episode, she says, "[Buffy] still thinks I'm little miss nobody, just her dumb little sister. Boy, is she in for a surprise." It's a deliciously ominous beat.

Throughout the season, a few of Glory's victims react to Dawn—their insanity makes them able to see her true form. Buffy and her mother learn who—or rather, *what*—Dawn really is in "No Place Like Home:"

MOΠK: The abomination found us. We had to hide the Key. Gave it form. Molded it flesh, made it human. And sent it to you.

BUFFY: Dawn.

MOΠK: … She is an innocent in this, and she needs you.

It's not until "Blood Ties" that Dawn discovers her true nature while on a snooping expedition with Spike, and she's completely blindsided. She freaks out, slashing her arms with a razor to see if she's truly human and will bleed (she does).

Of course, despite Buffy's best efforts, the narrative arc must move forward, and eventually Glory does capture Dawn and begin the ritual to bleed the Key and open the portal to one (of apparently many) hell dimension. According to lore, Dawn's blood will open the portal, and thus only Dawn's blood can close it again, and it briefly looks like Buffy will have to kill her sister.

She's prepared to do it if necessary (she *did* kill Angel to save the world once), but Buffy being, well, Buffy, she finds a workaround, referring back to the fact that the monks said they created Dawn from "Summers blood." Accordingly, it stands to reason that Buffy's own blood could close the portal just as well as Dawn's, and in the series' one hundredth episode, "The Gift," Buffy leaps into the portal herself, offering her own blood as the ultimate sacrifice. The episode ends with her devastated friends gathered around her grave. (Her fitting epigraph: "She saved the world. A lot.")

It's inevitable that Dawn's later storylines struggled to match the drama of season five, but in season seven, her feelings of rivalry with her Slayer sister come back into play, as one by one, Potential Slayers are brought into the house to live, train, and fight alongside Buffy . . . and Dawn remains stubbornly normal. In the aptly named "Potential," it briefly appears as though Dawn might actually be a Potential Slayer, after all; but ultimately, it's a case of mistaken identity, and it's a friend of hers who's been targeted instead.

Buffy is thrilled because it means her younger sister is no longer marked for a dangerous and most likely foreshortened life. But Xander is the one to comfort Dawn:

"They'll never know how tough it is, Dawnie. To be the one who *isn't* chosen; to live so near the spotlight and never step in it. But I know. I see more than anybody realizes, 'cause nobody's watching me. . . . You're not special. You're extraordinary."

—Xander, "Potential"

Love her or hate her, it must be said that Dawn does her best to help out, whether it be with research or errands or general moral support. For that alone, she definitely ranks higher in our hearts than your standard Cousin Oliver. Dawn serves to remind us that even "normal" human angst has real stakes (no pun intended) and that the struggle to accept one's own limitations can be as painful as any demon attack.

THE POTENTIALS

Season seven of *Buffy* has a mixed rep among fans and critics. Some argue that the show had run out of steam, its tone had shifted too much since moving networks, and it focused too heavily on the incredibly intense arc of Buffy being dragged out of heaven. It's true, our girl did come back with an extra helping of existential dread and burden, but we still maintain that season seven and the arrival of the Potentials is the perfect culmination of *Buffy*'s feminist promise.

When the final season premieres, the early episodes' cold opens feature young girls being stalked and killed without context. Soon we learn that these

are Potential Slayers, and they're being hunted by the Bringers on behalf of the First Evil to eliminate the Slayer line and thus any threat. Buffy, having graduated from naïve, reluctant foot soldier in season one to badass general in season seven, seeks out the remaining Potentials, protects them in her home, and trains them for battle. And then, with the help of Willow's magic, she empowers them with Slayer strength. They don't all survive the battle (some are killed in the battles leading up to the final confrontation). But they do all realize their full potential by the series end. And for once, a vampire Slayer's calling is no longer only, well, slaying.

Buffy tells the Potentials: "Every one of you, and girls we've never known, and generations to come . . . they will have strength they never dreamed of. And more than that, they will have each other" ("Potential").

As *Bustle* said, "[season seven] is all about girls from all over the world finding their inner goddesses . . . and kicking the tushies of their wannabe oppressors. It is literally young women fighting for their power and right to life; and every time I watch all the Potentials get Slayer strength, my heart grows about seven sizes."

Bustle had love for the actual Potentials themselves. "The large amount of silly teen girls who, just like Buffy did in the late nineties, stumbled into this new life as a potential Slayer are so fun. The slumber party vibe that takes over Buffy's house is a beautiful thing to see, and it really has no equal in any of the other seasons."

Hear! Hear!

Several of the Potentials are only seen in cold opens and are summarily dispatched. Some are seen in the finale montage wherein Willow activates their power. Very few are given particularly distinct personalities, with the exception of **KENNEDY** (activated), a spoiled, outspoken character who develops a relationship with Willow (and helps her while she's performing the activation spell), and **AMANDA** (activated), who plays *Dungeons and Dragons* with Andrew, Giles, and Xander the night before the final battle and who's killed in that battle.

Others are:

ANNABELLE—Vegetarian, preppy, flees Buffy's house before the final battle and is killed; Buffy buries her in the woods.

CARIDAD (activated)—After Buffy is expelled from the house, she joins Faith and some others to raid the Bringers' lair.

CHAO-AHN (activated)—Speaks only Cantonese, and her inability to communicate with the group is, in an oddly tone-deaf note, mostly used for comic relief.

CHLOE—Cannot handle the pressure and fear of the threat of the First; hangs herself.

COLLEEN (activated)—Featured in a sex dream Xander has about the Potentials in a less-empowered moment of the series; is notably played by Rachel Bilson of *The O.C.* fame.

DIANNE—Killed by Caleb when the team faces off against him in the vineyard.

DOMINIQUE (activated)—Is mentioned as having the flu at one point in her stay with Buffy.

EVE—Killed en route to Buffy by the Bringers, Eve still gets a moment to shine, so to speak, when the First takes her form and briefly infiltrates the group.

MOLLY—British, has a Cockney accent and uses British slang. Killed at the vineyard.

NORA—Murdered by the Bringers while under the care of a Watcher named Robson.

RONA (activated)—Sarcastic and pessimistic, Rona, black, is quick to mention to the extended group that "the black chick always gets it first" ("Potential"). Her arm is broken in battle at the vineyard, and she spends the rest of the series in a cast. Still, she fights valiantly in the final standoff at the Hellmouth, at one point using Buffy's enchanted scythe to take out several Turok-Han vampires.

SHANNON (activated)—Is picked up by Caleb while hitchhiking to Sunnydale; he attacks her and stabs her with a Bowie knife (giving her an unheard message to carry to Buffy), then throws her out of his car. She's found on the road by Faith and Willow and taken to the hospital.

VIOLET (activated)—One of the Potentials to have been identified by the Watchers' Council, she's been paired with a Watcher but has been sheltered until her arrival in Sunnydale. She tells the group she's never seen a vamp in person. She fights well even before being activated and joins Faith's raid on the vineyard. She survives the battle at the Hellmouth and helps tend a wounded Principal Wood.

FUN FACT: Felicia Day, the actress who portrays the potential Vi, went on to become an internet sensation with a cult following. In addition to working with Joss Whedon on *BtVS*, she also appeared in *Dollhouse* and *Dr. Horrible's Singalong Blog*. She launched her YouTube channel Geek & Sundry in 2009 and published a memoir, *You're Never Weird on the Internet (Almost)*, in 2015.

WHICH BADASS BABE ARE YOU?

If you're a Buffy fan, you definitely have your own ideas about favorite characters. You're shy and brainy, "such a Willow," or you're "having a Cordelia moment" when you make a petty comment. You're "slaying," a la Buffy, when you're kicking ass at life. Or maybe, like Cordelia, you "have layers" and can't be distilled down to one specific persona.

Or so you think.

Don't worry, you're in the hands of experts. Below we've provided a handy-dandy quiz to help you get in touch with your *Buffy* spirit babe. Bust out your number two pencils (pointy wooden things: always useful!) and get cracking!

1.   **The apocalypse has been prophesized. You:**

   A.   Run like the wind. Been there, done that. It's not exactly happy fun times.

   B.   Put your paper on Bosnia on hold and reluctantly help out with research.

   C.   Don your best gown and grab your crossbow. Let's do this.

   D.   A little web surfing, a little magic . . . you help in any way you can. And sometimes go for donuts.

   E.   Team up with the bad guys. They have more fun.

2. It's parent-teacher night at school. Where can we find you?

   A. You're, like, eleven hundred years old. You're home counting your money, duh.

   B. Naturally, you're part of the welcome committee. You got a blow-out and everything.

   C. You somehow got roped into the decorating committee because the principal's got a thing against you. But, bright side: you're around to stave off a vamp attack, if necessary.

   D. Helping with logistics and running damage control for friends who have less than stellar academic reps.

   E. Lolz. School? Hard pass.

3. What do you want to be when you grow up?

   A. Well, if you *have* to be a mortal human, you may as well get the Benjamins. So, something entrepreneurial.

   B. Trophy wife. Though you're willing to do more, like maybe to help your fellow man here and there (as long as he's not, like, smelly or gross).

   C. Do the words "sealed" and "fate" mean anything to you? Why go there? (But . . . maybe law enforcement? Or high school guidance counselor, if all else fails. Those kids really need a protector.)

   D. You've been unknowingly under the surveillance of a secret tech company that has made plans for you—and the one other person in your school who's equally smart. Plus, the gig comes with canapes.

   E. There's a decent chance you're going to operate outside the boundaries of the law. What of it?

4. Describe your personal style.

   A. Trendy, with a nod to heritage and tradition here and there (it's in the accessories, mostly).

   B. Lots of Lycra—if you've got it, flaunt it. Red and black are your signature colors, and woe to the person who tries to single white female your look.

   C. Forget practicality; if a fashion magazine told you to wear cats strapped to your feet, you'd probably do it. Proudly.

   D. Well, your mom used to dress you, but now that you're more independent, it's mostly lots of pink fuzz and shirts that make you look like a big birthday cake (that's the point).

   E. Black—leather, mostly. That, or you're sleeping nude.

5. **When it comes to romance, what's your type?**

    A. You've dated your share of bad boys over time (life is long, after all), but you have an embarrassing soft spot for dorky, basic, nerd-types.

    B. Generally speaking, you go for older guys with money, power . . . and cars.

    C. Your last boyfriend had a bicentennial. Sometimes you think passion and violence must be inextricably linked . . . Why is that?

    D. In the past, you've had a thing for cool, restrained musicians, but these days you're into women—mostly those with magic powers of some kind.

    E. Romance? Nah. Use 'em, abuse 'em, discard 'em. Assuming they can keep up . . .

6. **What are some of your fave hobbies and/or extracurriculars?**

    A. You work retail to earn cash for goods and service. Yay, capitalism!

    B. Ugh. No, thanks. House, hotel, hotel, husband. Nothing's going to get in the way of *that* dream.

    C. You have, like, zero free time. But when you do have a rare minute to chill, it's all about the retail therapy or vegging with your friends watching eighties' movies and eating pineapple pizza and chocolate.

    D. Poking around online (though chatting with strangers on the internet has gone badly in the past), studying the black arts.

    E. Blowing off steam with a random boy toy at the local club.

7. **Do you have a beauty routine?**

    A. You were immortal for so long, you never needed one. But you change it up with your hair for fun these days.

    B. Obvi. And get your mitts off the $40 hairspray—it's imported.

    C. You for sure care about your appearance. You once spent all your allowance on a new crème rinse that was neither crème-y nor rinse-y, which was an unfortunate life lesson.

    D. You've threatened to change up your look, but the most you've done is cut your hair short senior year.

    E. You're a straight-up smokeshow, naturally. But you can't resist a dark lipstick when you see it.

8. **Are you close with your family?**

    A. Most of your family's been dead for a few millennia, but you have one or two ride-or-die friends.

    B. Your parents are afraid of you . . . as well they should be.

    C. You would die for them. Come to think of it, you *have* died for them.

    D. Your parents aren't super-aware of your extracurricular activities . . . or your activities in general, really. They don't really get you.

    E. What family? You're real Spartan. It's you against the world.

9. **Favorite subject in school?**

    A. Anything but math. You're flunking math.

    B. You actually do well in all of your classes, but you keep it on the DL to maintain your rep as "it girl."

    C. You were digging your psych class for a while . . . the TA was a muffin, too.

    D. In high school, you subbed for the comp sci teacher when she was running late.

    E. Does cutting class count?

10. **What's your personal motto?**

    A. "I like my money the way it is . . . When it's mine."

    B. "When it comes to dating, *I'm* the Slayer."

    C. "If the apocalypse comes, beep me."

    D. "Don't warn the tadpoles!"

    E. "Want. Take. Have."

RESULTS:

Time to tally your scores and own your inner *Buffy* babe. Are you ready? If you got:

Mostly As:

ANYA: You're brash, you're blunt, and you value the almighty dollar above all else. You've been around the block, and you have a jaded but realistic view of mankind: men are evil, and accordingly, there's little you love more than vengeance. Other priorities: personal boundaries and orgasms. You're terrified of bunnies, and you'll fight the good fight when all is said and done. But you'll be *very* sarcastic about it.

Mostly Bs:

CORDELIA: You're smart, beautiful, and totally un-mess-with-able. Girls want to be you, and guys want to be with you—you know it, and you have been known to exploit it to your own advantage. Could you stand to be a little, well, nicer? Maybe. But to what end? You're resourceful and resilient and proud to hold the title of Reigning Champion, Bitch of the Year.

Mostly Cs:

BUFFY: What you wouldn't give to be destiny-free: shopping, hanging with your friends, or—gosh, even studying. But you have to save the world, again. A sacred duty can be a real drag, but you're a born warrior and leader, and when the moment arrives, you make the hard choices. You love breakfast food and boys that aren't always great for you. You have a knack for wordplay. Also, you look cute in a tiara.

Mostly Ds:

WILLOW: You're shy and helpless . . . or so you let people think. Truth is, knowledge is power, and you're hella-smart. You know your way around a magic shop and have been called a Big Bad and also a Goddess by those who've seen the depths of your skills (these days, you use your powers for good). You're a loyal friend, a partner, and you're open-minded about your sexual orientation. You have frog fear, but so what?

Mostly Es:

FAITH: You don't break the rules—you make up your own, and anyone who doesn't like it can stay out of your way. The world has mostly disappointed you, so you tend not to rely on anyone but yourself. You *love* being strong, and you fly by the seat of your pants. Sometimes this has consequences, but you make like you don't care. Newsflash: you might not be as tough as you think you are. (You are, however, as crazy hot as you say.)

PART II:

HOW TO KILL IT, *BUFFY BABE–STYLE*

If you're reading this book, chances are it's because you're a fan of Buffy, her universe, and her patented brand of girl power. As such, we probably don't need to persuade you that there are valuable life lessons to be found in every episode.

Well, maybe we don't *need* to persuade you. But we're sure as Slayage going to spend some time talking about the meaningful takeaways that *Buffy* (and Buffy) have to offer. Grab a pen, flip open your Slayer handbook, and have a hang.

"If one man can destroy everything,
why can't one girl change it?"

—Malala Yousafzai

NOT EVERYTHING
IS ABOUT KISSING...

. . . some stuff is about groping. (But Buffy and Willow know the value of smoochies.)

DON'T BE AFRAID TO TAKE CHARGE

GILES: I'll put myself in your hands.

JENNY: That sounds like fun.

—"Lie to Me"

We live in the modern world, thankfully, when it's much more acceptable (and even expected) for women to take their sexuality into their own hands. Case in point: Faith steering Xander around the curves, and Willow initiating her first kiss with Oz when he's going slower than she'd like (as per the previous page, she wants the smoochies!). Get it, ladies—it's about time.

"We need to reshape our own perception of how we view ourselves. We have to step up as women and take the lead."

—Beyoncé

STAND BY YOUR MAN
(OR WOMAN, OR VAMP)

"You can attack me, you can send assassins after me, that's fine. But nobody messes with my boyfriend."

—Buffy, "What's My Line, Part 2"

A good partner has her stud-muffin's back. Buffy's had to exact revenge on behalf of her honeys more than once (Owen, Angel . . . heck, she's even gone to bat for Spike on occasion). Even Cordelia stands up for Xander when her bitchy girlfriends give her grief for dating a dork (though she does still call him "lame" in the process). Willow, of course, is so committed to Tara that when Tara is killed, she turns full-dark-no-stars in a revenge gambit. (To be fair, she arguably took that one too far.)

VALUE YOURSELF, GIRL

WILLOW : You know, I have a choice. I can spend my life waiting for Xander to go out with every other girl in the world until he notices me. Or I can just get on with my life.

BUFFY : Good for you!

WILLOW : Well, I didn't choose yet . . .

—"Inca Mummy Girl"

And it maybe takes her a weensy bit longer after this conversation, but Willow *does* choose: when she meets Oz and senses their chemistry, she goes for it, no longer content to pine for a guy who's kept her in the friend zone for ages.

This can be a tricky one, though. We get it, and we've all been there. When Angel loses his soul, it takes Buffy some time to recognize that her boyfriend is gone. She can't bring herself to kill him right away. (Okay, maybe we haven't been *there*, but we've all had trouble getting over a bad boy.) She also mopes after Parker, a college sleaze who seduces her and drops her. "I think you're missing something about the poop-head principle," Willow tells her when Buffy wonders if the two of them might eventually be able to make it work ("The Harsh Light of Day"). And Harmony lets Spike debase her even though she knows she's worth more. Sometimes it's hard to make the grown-up, mature choice, and sometimes it's hard to recognize our own self-worth. But our Buffy babes get there in the end . . . and you can, too.

"I myself have never been able to find out precisely what feminism is: I only know that people call me a feminist whenever I express sentiments that differentiate me from a doormat."

—Dame Rebecca West

LOVE IS COMPLICATED...

BUFFY: I just get messed sometimes. I wish we could be regular kids.

ANGEL: I'll never be a kid.

BUFFY: All right, a regular kid and her cradle-robbing, creature-of-the-night boyfriend.

—"What's My Line, Part One"

The thing is, there's no such thing as "regular." We all carry our own baggage and our own experiences with us wherever we go. Does that mean we don't deserve love or can't make love happen? Of course not. We can be complicated people, so it would stand to reason that our relationships can be complicated, too. It's a question of finding a partner whose baggage matches (or, better yet, complements) your own.

...AND CRAZY-MAKING

"Love makes you do the wacky," Buffy says, referring to her flirtatious dancing with Xander that she does only to make Angel jealous ("Some Assembly Required"). Cordelia's love for Xander makes her nearly a completely different person. Certainly she taps into a kinder, gentler spirit. Willow has feelings for Xander even in the midst of a happy, healthy relationship with Oz. Love is deep, love is *blood*, as Spike says, and accordingly, it inspires all the biggest feels in our gals (and in our own hearts).

FUN FACT: Sarah Michelle Gellar has revealed in interviews that she's Team Angel rather than Team Spike.

WE ARE ALL COOKIE DOUGH, WAITING TO BAKE

"I always figured there was something wrong with me, you know, because I couldn't make it work. But maybe I'm not supposed to. . . . Because, okay: I'm cookie dough. I'm not done baking. I'm not finished becoming whoever the hell it is I'm gonna turn out to be. I make it through this, and the next thing, and the next thing, and maybe one day, I turn around and realize I'm ready. I'm cookies."

—Buffy, "Chosen"

Buffy's epiphany here is that, up until now, she's been waiting for the right relationship to make her feel whole. But the thing is, if we're not whole on our own, there's no way we can be whole with someone else. Does that mean we have to have our lives 100 percent together before we're ready to be in a healthy relationship? Of course not. But we do have to know who we are and what we stand for, which means we can't go into a relationship half-baked.

For Buffy, it took the third (or is it fourth?) pending apocalypse to bring about this revelation. Here's your gentle nudge before things get so dire.

GET WITH THE TIMES

"I was brought up a proper lady. I wasn't meant to understand things. I'm just meant
 to look pretty, and then someone nice will marry me."

—Buffy, "Halloween"

Of course, our girl would never say such a thing if she were in her right mind,
and this quote comes from the episode "Halloween," where she wears an
old-fashioned costume in a gambit to surprise Angel as one of the noblewomen
straight out of his adolescence. When a curse makes her *become* the simpering
damsel in distress, she's reminded of just how awesome agency and kicking
ass actually feel. It's 2019, ladies (and gentlemen and all of us everywhere on
the gender spectrum)—traditional gender roles are *way* passe.

"Of course I am not worried about
intimidating men. The type of man
who will be intimidated by me is exactly
the type of man I have no interest in."

—Chimamanda Ngozi Adichie

AND SPEAKING OF ABANDONING CLICHÉS...

JENNY: Did anyone ever tell you you're kind of a fuddy duddy?

GILES: Nobody ever seems to tell me anything else.

JENNY: Did anyone ever tell you you're kind of a sexy fuddy duddy?

GILES: No, actually, that part usually gets left out. I can't imagine why.

—"The Dark Age"

Again, it's 2019—even the cis-norm-identifying among us don't need to be totally rigid or predictable in our gender roles, and no one needs anymore toxic masculinity in their life. The prototypical alpha male is super outdated—Jenny was saying so before it was cool.

And while sometimes it may seem that, as Faith says, "all men are beasts," Buffy tells her, "You can trust some guys. Really. I've read about them." Swap out "guys" for "potential partners," and we might be onto something.

SEX CAN BE MEANINGFUL...

... though it doesn't necessarily *have* to be. When Willow loses her virginity to Oz, she comments afterward that she feels different. Buffy, on the other hand, muses to Willow, "What I'm wondering is, does this always happen? Sleep with a guy and he goes all evil?" ("The Harsh Light of Day")

Of course, that's a huge cliché, too, and it doesn't have to be that way (no matter who you're sleeping with). If it's fun and you're responsible and consenting, go on with your bad self. But know that sex *can* result in capital-f-Feelings, and that some people aren't going to be as thoughtful with your feelings as you might like. Choose your partners with care and self-respect. Under the right circumstances, as Anya says, sex can be "like a party for our aliveness."

A GOOD RELATIONSHIP IS BUILT ON ACCEPTING ONE ANOTHER

Accept your partner for who they are. Even if "who they are" happens to be a werewolf, sometimes. As Willow says to Oz, "You're nice, and you're funny, and you don't smoke, and okay, werewolf, but that's not all the time. I mean, three days out of the month, I'm not much fun to be around, either" ("Phases"). And those two kids had a pretty good run. Look, nobody's perfect—a healthy relationship will make space for people's quirks and foibles and allow people to bring out the best in each other.

HEARTACHE IS UTTER PAIN

Yes, relationships end. We've all been there, and we've all been nearly blinded by the loss. The only way out is through. As Buffy observes when Willow is grieving Oz's departure:

BUFFY: I've never seen her like this before, Giles. It's like it hurts too much to even form words.

GILES: But you've felt that way yourself, and you got through it.

BUFFY: Well, I ran away and went to hell—and then I got through it. I'm kind of hoping Willow won't use me as a model.

—**"Something Blue"**

Willow *does* get through her breakup—as do Buffy, Cordy, Anya, and others throughout the series' run. The common thread seems to mostly be leaning on your friends.

HEALTHY LOVE
DOESN'T *HAVE* TO
HAVE DRAMA

It's easy to get swept up in conflict, but the truth is, usually high drama isn't a sign of passion but rather dysfunction. "I love being around Riley," Buffy says. "But I still feel like something's missing." "He's not making you miserable?" Willow asks. "Exactly!" Buffy says.

"I can't help thinking, isn't that where the fire comes from? Can a nice, safe relationship be that intense? It's nuts, but part of me believes that real love and passion *have* to go hand-in-hand with lots of pain and fighting."

—Buffy, "Something Blue"

Yes, Buffy. It *is* nuts. It makes for great TV drama, but in real life, it's pretty unproductive. Thankfully, Buffy does eventually come around to realize this. Talking about vampires, she says, "Sex and death and love and pain: It's all the same damn thing to you." Her normal, human self has come to understand that sex and love don't have to equal pain. (She just needed to be fully baked to get there.)

TEACHER'S PET
School, Learning, and Knowledge

"The most courageous act is to think for yourself. Aloud."

—Coco Chanel

KNOWLEDGE IS POWER

Xander says this as a joke, but the ladies know he's right. Buffy is often too busy kicking demon butt to stay totally on top of her studies, but research skills are integral to her process. She knows well enough to outsource this to her brainy buds—generally, Willow—when necessary. And although she may be struggling in some of her classes, she's no dummy: the Slayer's SAT scores reveal stealth smarts, and she understands this probably means more options for her, life-wise. The characters on *Buffy* all take different approaches to school and learning, but every one of them has his or her own area of expertise and body of knowledge. We could all learn from them (pun intended).

NERDS ARE IN

Cordelia tries to hide her good grades and high test scores, and in this one area, she's sadly off-trend: geek is chic, and Willow is the queen of the clever-cute. Girls who study are hot, as *Buffy* demonstrates time and time again.

"Girls should never be afraid to be smart."

—Emma Watson

BE EFFICIENT

"I don't think anyone should have to do anything educational in school if they don't want to."

—Cordelia, "Some Assembly Required"

Cordelia's science fair project (when she poses the question "Tomato: vegetable or fruit?") may seem like a cop-out, but when the top science student is creating a *reanimated person made of stitched-together body parts*? You probably never stood a chance. Sometimes, good enough really is good enough. No need to spend more time on a project than absolutely necessary. It's important to know where and when to expend your energy for maximum efficiency. Buffy's delegation of tasks is another example of this principle in action.

"Is the world ending? I have to research a paper on Bosnia for tomorrow, but if the world's ending, I'm not gonna bother."

—Cordelia, "Helpless"

It's all about priorities.

LOVE YOUR LIBRARY

BUFFY: See, this is a school, and we have students, and they check out books, and then they learn things.

GILES: I was beginning to suspect that was a myth.

—"Never Kill a Boy on the First Date"

Buffy's Slayer education takes place mostly in the school library, which quickly becomes her happy place, her safe place, and her number-one after-hours hang. We civilians would do well to take our cues. In the age of the internet, it's easy (but totally misguided!) to argue that libraries are obsolete, but there's no cyber-substitute for the community haven the library provides: educational resources, programming, and a place for parents to bring kids for free (and wholesome) entertainment. If you haven't already, get thee a library card.

The library: it's where the books live.

It may be that your school or town library has been overtaken by demon-fighting superheroes—we feel you. In that case, consider this point as being a case for lifelong learning and the library itself a metaphor. Whatever your passion, locate the relevant inner sanctum (The ocean? A yoga studio? A woodshop?), and make your space to learn, evolve, and create.

FIERCE READS

A Killer Collection

Bad Feminist: Essays, Roxane Gay

The Handmaid's Tale, Margaret Atwood

Becoming, Michelle Obama

Gender Outlaw: On Men, Women, and the Rest of Us, Kate Bornstein

Men Explain Things to Me, Rebecca Solnit

She Persisted: 13 American Women Who Changed the World, Chelsea Clinton

The Female Persuasion: A Novel, Meg Wolitzer

The Color Purple, Alice Walker

Little Women, Louisa May Alcott

I Dissent: Ruth Bader Ginsburg Makes Her Mark, Debbie Levy

Sadie, Courtney Summers

Goodnight Stories for Rebel Girls: 100 Tales of Extraordinary Women, Elena Favilli and Francesca Cavallo

Persepolis: The Story of a Childhood, Marjane Satrapi

The Burn for Burn Trilogy, Jenny Han and Siobhan Vivian

Sex Object: A Memoir, Jessica Valenti

Here We Are: Feminism for the Real World, Kelly Jensen (ed.)

Rad Women Worldwide: Artists and Athletes, Pirates and Punks, and Other Revolutionaries Who Shaped History, Kate Schatz

Slayer, Kiersten White

The Buffy the Vampire Slayer Encyclopedia: The Ultimate Guide to the Buffyverse, Nancy Holder and Lisa Clancy

QUESTION AUTHORITY

"A lot of educators tell students, 'Think of your principal as your pal.' I say, think of me as your judge, jury, and executioner."

—Principal Snyder, "School Hard"

Buffy's had some wonderful, nurturing teachers, but she's also dealt with a bunch of school administrators who were emphatically *not* on her side, occasionally were outright working against her, or who just plain didn't get her. Though she always did her best to show respect, she also knew when to go with her gut and disregard what a teacher or principal might be telling her. Know thyself, trust thyself. Be respectful, but question the system and the powers that be (literal and metaphorical).

"Women are the real architects of society."

—Harriet Beecher Stowe

TECHNOLOGY IS HERE TO STAY

"Well, evil just compounds evil, doesn't it? First, I'm sentenced to a computer tutorial on Saturday. Now I have to read some computer book. There are books on computers? Isn't the point of computers to replace books?"

—Cordelia, "The Dark Age"

No, Cordy. Computers can't *replace* books. But they aren't going anywhere, either. The cyberworld gives us access to communities and resources we might otherwise never have known. (Ms. Calendar starts a Wiccan power circle online, which is way metaphysical and super cool.) That being said, anyone can be anything on the internet, so if you're making friends online, stay safe and vet your new acquaintances. Women are vulnerable enough when dating without adding an extra element of the unknown into the mix.

XANDER: When are we going to have to use computers in real life, anyway?

JENNY: Let's see, there's home, school, work, games—

—"The Dark Age"

THINK OUTSIDE THE CLASSROOM

XANDER: Buffy, this isn't just about looking at a bunch of animals. This is about not being in class.

BUFFY: You're right. Suddenly the animals look shiny and new.

—"The Pack"

Buffy may be talking about a field trip to the zoo, and sure, she may be employing killer levels of sarcasm, but she's not wrong. Learning doesn't have to take place in a classroom, and it doesn't have to be super linear or traditional. Experiential wisdom is as valuable as anything to be found in books as long as you're careful not to accidentally allow yourself to be possessed by the spirit of a hyena (hate it when that happens).

. . . AND THINK LONG-TERM

XANDER: Why do I need to learn this?

WILLOW: 'Cause otherwise you'll flunk math. You remember: you fail math, you flunk out of school, you end up being the guy at the pizza place that sweeps the floor and says, "Hey, kids, where's the cool parties this weekend?"

—"The Pack"

Education = opportunities. And like Cordelia says, with options, you can, among other things "leave Sunnydale and never come back."

"I know high school can be frustrating. But if you just get through it, then you can go to college or join the French Foreign Legion or anything you want."

—Buffy, "Help"

Interesting suggestions there, but duly noted.

BROADEN YOUR HORIZONS

"You know what's so cool about college? The diversity. You've got rich people and you've got . . . all the other people."

—Cordelia, "Reptile Boy"

Another argument for higher education.

DO WELL, ATTRACT OPPORTUNITY

"I got in! To colleges. Real live colleges. And now they're wooing me. They're pitching woo!"

—Willow, "Choices"

Willow's hard work pays off when she is not only accepted to college but has her pick among a bunch of great options, all of which are competing to have her. Don't underestimate the appeal of the snack options, too.

BUFFY: I can't believe you got into Oxford. That's where they make Gileses!

WILLOW: I know! I could learn and have scones!

—"Choices"

WORKING HARD IS HARD WORK

"I thought it was gonna be more like in the movies. You know, inspirational music and a montage: me sharpening pencils, reading, writing, falling asleep on a big pile of books with my glasses all crooked, because in the montage I have glasses. Real life is so slow, and it hurts my occipital lobe."

—Buffy, "Out of My Mind"

Okay, sure, that's the thing—work is, um, well, *work*. Don't let that fact take you by surprise or daunt you. It will ultimately be worth it.

"In high school, knowledge was pretty much frowned upon. You really had to work to learn anything. But here, I mean, the energy, the collective intelligence—it's like this force, this penetrating force; I can feel my mind just opening up, you know, letting the place just thrust into it and . . . spurt knowledge . . . into . . . That sentence ended up in a different place than it started out in."

—Willow, "The Freshman"

I mean, we know what she means.

IT'S ALL THE "REAL WORLD"

"Why do people who don't go to college always refer to everything outside of college as the 'real world'? Like college is some imaginary realm with elves and witches and . . . Huh."

—Willow, "Tough Love"

Your college experience—if you had or plan on having one—is probably very different from Willow's. But even *sans* elves, I think we can make the case that "real" life is the one you're living, whichever path you chose, and that there are ramifications and consequences that come from the choices we make and the motivations behind these decisions.

KNOWLEDGE IS ITS OWN REWARD

"Now [Professor Walsh] wants me to lead a discussion group next class. Which means more work, right? Shouldn't she have a better reward system? Like a cookie?"

—Buffy, "Wild at Heart"

Not every teacher is going to provide cookies (in fact, most probably won't!). Identify your own best motivator—chocolate, a coffee date with a friend, a well-earned Netflix binge—and make sure you stay on top of self-care. You deserve it! (And feel free to BYO cookies if that's your reward of choice.)

PLAY LIKE A GIRL

Your Ultimate Girl-Power Soundtrack

"Run the World (Girls)," Beyoncé

"Confident," Demi Lovato

"The Greatest," Sia

"Roar," Katy Perry

"Express Yourself," Madonna

"Just a Girl," No Doubt

"Bossy," Kelis

"Rebel Girl," Bikini Kill

"You Don't Own Me," Lesley Gore

"Bitch," Meredith Brooks

"Respect," Aretha Franklin

"Flawless," Beyoncé

"These Boots Are Made for Walkin'," Nancy Sinatra

"Work It," Missy Elliott

"I'm Every Woman," Whitney Houston

"Worth It," Fifth Harmony

"Control," Janet Jackson

"Miss Independent," Kelly Clarkson

"Bad Girls," M.I.A.

"Army of Me," Björk

"Hollaback Girl," Gwen Stefani

LIES MY PARENTS TOLD ME

On Family—Blood and Found

MOTHER CAN'T KNOW BEST IF YOU DON'T TALK TO HER

This being *Buffy*, much of the interpersonal (or, more to the point, interfamily) interaction is about deception. For starters, as we've mentioned, Joss is a sucker for heartache. But beyond that there's the inherent dishonesty that comes from being a Slayer—if ever a teen had something about her innermost self that she felt needed hiding . . .

For that reason, much of Buffy's relationship with her mother (her father being essentially a nonpresence on the show, which is a statement in and of itself) is characterized by conflict and secrecy. And they have many of the typical mother-daughter fights: Buffy wanting to dress in clothes Joyce thinks are inappropriate, Buffy wanting to stay out later than Joyce would like (never mind that she's fighting vamps).

JOYCE: A little responsibility, Buffy. That's all I ask. Honestly, don't you ever think about anything besides boys and clothes?

BUFFY: Saving the world from vampires.

JOYCE: I swear, sometimes I have no idea what goes on in your head.

—"Bad Eggs"

When Buffy does finally come out to her mother as Slayer, it takes Joyce some time to absorb the information in a low-key nod to other forms of coming out (in fact, when Willow *does* come out to Buffy, in season four, the Slayer responds much more smoothly than Joyce does about Buffy's calling).

Willow, too, feels misunderstood by her mother, who refers to adolescence in psycho-babble and seems to consider Willow only within the context of such. "I'm not an age group, Mom. I'm me. Willow group," she tells her mother, in "Gingerbread," only to be outed as a witch . . . and nearly burned

at the stake by a gaggle of spellbound Sunnydale mothers—including, yes, her own.

As the series evolves, Buffy is more open with her mother, and in time, Joyce comes to accept Buffy's role as the Slayer, even if she hates its inherent danger.

In the Buffyverse, as in life, mother-and-daughter relationships are complicated. People are complicated. But they can love each other—and well—with a little honesty and effort.

LOVING YOUR FOUND FAMILY

Buffy is all about found family: although the Slayer and her Scoobies often feel alienated from their loved ones, they make their own blood ties through their loyalty to one another. When Tara's family shows up in town to terrorize her and drag her back home (where, it's implied, they'll subjugate her, as they've done to the women in their family for generations), Buffy is the first to step forward. "Who the hell are you?" Tara's father demands.

Buffy's response? "We're family." ("Family")

Friends, made family . . . In Dawn's case, *literally* "made." Though she's been created to exist as Buffy's fourteen-year-old sister, she's actually only been around for six months. But blood is blood, Buffy tells her, in "Blood Ties." In this case, the familial link transcends the magic that was used to manufacture it. "It doesn't matter how you got here or where you came from. You are my sister. There's no way you could annoy me as much if you weren't," Buffy says, pointing out that the monks made Dawn from Summers blood.

PARENTING MEANS LETTING GO

Once Joyce is gone, Buffy has to step up as a surrogate mother to Dawn. In fact, all of the Scoobies act as a fluid, dynamic alternative to the traditional—and outdated—nuclear family, with Willow and Tara frequently stepping in as mothers, too.

Dawn chafes at being protected from danger and constantly shielded; she thinks her big sister is treating her like a baby. Buffy explains to her friends that she's trying to give Dawn the "normal life" she herself could never have. She's even a little jealous, resenting the fact that Dawn gets to be a kid in a way Buffy never did. In season six's "Grave," though, the two fight side

by side, and when the battle is over, Buffy realizes she's underestimated her little sister—who isn't all that little anymore. "I got it so wrong," Buffy says. "I don't want to protect you from the world—I want to show it to you." Just as Joyce had to give Buffy space to carry out her Slayer duties, so Buffy needed to let Dawn grow and flourish.

SISTERS DO IT FOR EACH OTHER

Buffy's not the only protective Summers sister. Dawn is not kidding around when she threatens Spike:

"You sleep, right? . . . I can't take you in a fight or anything, even with that chip in your head. But you do sleep. And if you hurt my sister *at all* . . . you're gonna wake up on fire."

—"Beneath You"

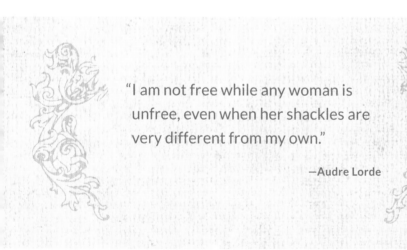

"I am not free while any woman is unfree, even when her shackles are very different from my own."

—Audre Lorde

YOU'VE GOT A FRIEND

Financial independence, good, but on *Buffy*, people need people. Human (and sometimes demon) connection is often what *saves* the characters. In the same way that we make our own found family, we build our villages with our friends. From the moment Willow tells Buffy "We're, like, the Slayerettes," Buffy's bond with her buds becomes unbreakable. In fact, in season four, Adam's attempts to destroy Buffy begin with trying to get between the Slayer and her friends. It's only when they reconcile and join forces that they can beat him.

Buffy reflects often on the loneliness and isolation of Slayerdom; it's clear that her friends keep her grounded. By contrast, Faith is distrustful and rejects any attempts that the Scoobies make to reach out to her. Her betrayal of Buffy quickly erodes any goodwill the gang might have extended her way.

"It didn't have to be this way, but you made your choice," Willow tells her after Faith has defected to Team Mayor. "I know you've had a tough life. I know some people think you've had a lot of bad breaks and that you've hardened your heart to protect yourself from the pain . . . Well, boohoo. Poor you. You had a lot more in your life than some people. You had friends like Buffy. Now you've got no one." ("Choices")

And even a hero with a sacred duty knows that a life without friends is unbearable.

WHAT'S MY LINE?

THE WHOLE "CAREER" THING

DO THE WORDS "SEALED" AND "FATE" MEAN ANYTHING TO YOU?

Buffy and her friends don't lack for ambition, and in season three in particular, when they're applying to colleges and considering life after Sunnydale, they discuss big-picture career stuff. But it's hard for Buffy in particular to think long-term, since her sacred duty comes first and she believes it always will.

BUFFY: No matter what my aptitude test says, we already know my deal.

XANDER: Yep, high risk, subminimum wage . . .

BUFFY: Pointy wooden things . . .

—"What's My Line"

But that doesn't mean she doesn't sometimes wonder. And if nothing else, our girl's certainly open to options. In season six, when she's struggling to keep the household running after Joyce dies, she tries several jobs: construction with Xander, retail at Giles's and Anya's magic shop . . . nothing quite sticks, but that's mostly due to a weird little spell the Trio cast to disorient her (spoiler alert: it works).

Eventually, Buffy takes a job as a server at Doublemeat Palace, which is degrading. ("My hat has a cow," she mumbles, when ex Riley pops in unannounced, "As You Were.") She needs a paycheck, and she's not too proud to work an unskilled job.

Dawn recognizes the injustice of Buffy not being able to be compensated fairly, given the magnitude of what she does. (In fact, it's Anya who, in "Flooded," suggests that Buffy charge people for slaying.) "You can't charge innocent people for saving their lives," Dawn protests, even knowing, "Buffy's never gonna be a lawyer. Or a doctor. Anything big." Being the

Slayer may be "way bigger," as Xander points out, but it doesn't pay the bills.

It's an interesting reflection on the sacrifices we make as adults to build sustainable lives while also balancing our passions and our personal callings. It's not always romantic, but it's life.

GET IT DONE

The Slayer is nothing if not pragmatic, though, as we see from the simple fact of her taking the gig at Doublemeat. Other *Buffy* babes are similarly practicality-minded: Cordelia takes a job as a sales clerk when her father is indicted for tax fraud and her family loses their money. After she leaves *Buffy*, she heads to L.A., and it's through her own gumption that Angel Investigations eventually turns a profit.

And let's not forget Anya, who loves nothing more than to earn her own paycheck. After landing a job with Giles at the Magic Shop, she says, "I'm just so excited! They come in, I help them. They give me money in exchange for goods. You give me money for working for you. I have a place in the world now. I'm part of the system. I'm a workin' gal!" ("Family")

Anya may be blunt, and it's possible her focus on money is a little . . . intense . . . but she knows what all smart feminists know: financial independence is key.

"I didn't get there by wishing for it or hoping for it, but by working for it."

—Estée Lauder

BEAUTY AND THE BEAST

Looking and Feeling Your Best—
By Yourself, for Yourself

GIRLIE THINGS

It's no secret that the pressure on women to look good—that is, to reflect traditional, patriarchal, Westernized beauty norms at all times, at any cost— is, in a word, *bananas.* You'd think the Slayer would be exempt from worrying about the male gaze, but alas, even ushering in a new brand of girl power, Buffy—and *Buffy*—traded on the stereotypical cultural beauty norms. So, in a world where young women are *literally* being stitched together piecemeal to create the perfect girlfriend, what does *Buffy* have to teach us about embracing the girlie?

For starters—that "typical" girls can be dangerous.

FASHION IS FUN

"Shopping was a major theme," Buffy says of her summer vacation ("When She Was Bad"), when she meets up again with Xander and Willow. It's relaxing. It's a hobby. No shame. Remember: never underestimate the girlie girl. It's entirely possible she has power you can't begin to fathom.

"I look cute in a tiara," Buffy says while loading a rifle ("Homecoming"). It's not a paradox; it's just her.

"For I conclude that the enemy is not lipstick, but guilt itself; we deserve lipstick, if we want it, AND free speech; we deserve to be sexual AND serious—or whatever we please. We are entitled to wear cowboy boots to our own revolution."

—Naomi Wolf

DRESS THE PART

"I like your dress," the Master tells Buffy after he's killed her ("Prophecy Girl"). He's not the only one. *Everyone* has something to say about that iconic white gown, and arguably, our girl stands a little taller when she's wearing it. Is it the most practical ensemble for demon-busting? Maybe not. But Buffy feels good in it, and feeling good goes a long way toward putting your best foot forward.

Bonus: Once the Master's dust, she's ready to party.

See also: Buffy's quick change into a killer lilac prom gown after dispatching of a bunch of Devil Dogs.

OWN YOUR LOOK AND BE ORIGINAL

Cordelia not only has to have the most expensive item, but she'll terrorize anyone who dares show up in the same outfit she's wearing. "This is what happens when you sign those free trade agreements!" she shrieks, seeing another girl wearing her Todd Oldham ("Bad Eggs").

Cordy takes it too far, obvi—but if you've got a thing, make it yours, own it, and keep it distinct. As the throw pillow says: "Be yourself; everyone else is already taken" (actually a quote from Oscar Wilde).

"Never dull your shine for anyone else."

—Tyra Banks

THERE'S ALWAYS TIME
FOR AESTHETICS

Look, just because you're Slaying demons doesn't mean you can't care about your appearance. In "Prophecy Girl," Buffy bemoans breaking a nail, imploring a distracted Giles to care. Even young Dawn knows the score:

"I bet there's tons of stuff like this, procedures we can use that don't involve magic spells, just good solid detective work. Like, we could develop a database of tooth impressions and demon-skin samples. And I could wear high heels more."

"Wow, that was so close to being empowering," Buffy tells her, to which Dawn simply replies, "Well, everyone wants a slender ankle" ("Same Time, Same Place").

Look—she's not wrong.

> "Pour yourself a drink, put on some lipstick, and pull yourself together."
>
> —Elizabeth Taylor

LEATHER IS COOL

It just is. Faith's leather pants may be shorthand for "evil Slayer," but when Buffy steps into her iconic red leather pants at the close of season three, it's all business. The Slayer has put aside some of her frillier, girlier concerns and toughened up.

Even Dawn admits leather is cool. It's why she briefly harbors a semi-crush on Spike, however ill-advised that may be.

HAVE A LITTLE PERSPECTIVE

Male gaze aside, looking good leads to feeling good and, overall, can be instrumental in helping us all slay. But let's be sure to keep a clear head about the role fashion plays.

CORDELIA: It stays with you forever. No matter what they tell you, none of that rust and blood and grime comes out. I mean, you can dry-clean till Judgment Day, you are living with those stains.

JENNY: Yes. That's the worst part of being hung upside down by a vampire that wants to slit your throat. The stains.

CORDELIA: I hear you.

—"When She Was Bad"

Cordy may be a fashion "do" 90 percent of the time, but ladies? All the nope. Every now and then it's okay to let your fashion sense slip when there are more important issues at stake (pun fully intended).

"I would rather be a bad feminist than no feminist at all."

—Roxane Gay

BAD GIRLS

Authority, Agency, Power, and Generally Killing It

KNOW YOUR WORTH

Buffy is a Slayer. For a while, she's *the* Slayer, in point of fact. She knows it, she owns it, and she doesn't let anyone tell her otherwise. We may be mere mortals, but we could take a page from the Buffster.

RILEY : No weapons. No backup. You don't go after a demon that size by yourself.

BUFFY : I do.

—"Doomed"

And she does. Again, and again, and again. As she herself says, "I can beat up demons until the cows come home, and then I can beat up the cows" ("Intervention").

"I am a woman with thoughts and questions and shit to say. I say if I'm beautiful. I say if I'm strong. You will not determine my story—I will."

—Amy Schumer

...AND DON'T BE AFRAID TO LET OTHERS KNOW

Time and again, not only does Buffy have to own her own awesomeness, but she has to make sure that others understand just how much ass she kicks, too. Women are often hesitant to speak up on their own behalves. We've been socialized to devalue our own skills and give others credit that's really ours. Buffy knows better than that. She's a full-on warrior, and by the time the series concludes, she takes orders from no one. And she isn't shy about it.

In fact, even when she temporarily loses her memory due to a misguided spell of Willow's, she reacts to a demon attack instinctively and quickly realizes her own strength. "I think I know why Joan's the boss," she tells the others. "I'm like a superhero or something" ("Tabula Rasa").

A Slayer by any other name still slays, friends.

MAKE YOUR REBELLION COUNT

Buffy turning her back on the Council? Excellent use of autonomy. Dawn going through a klepto phase and stealing a mother-of-pearl toothbrush? Uh, misguided at best.

BUFFY: You stole a *toothbrush*. As rebellious teenagers go, you're kinda square.

DAWN: Dental hygiene is important.

—"Entropy"

It *is*. And yet . . . rebels without a cause (or at least, causes more important than healthy gums) don't often go on to do big things.

Women belong in all places where decisions are being made . . . It shouldn't be that women are the exception."

—Ruth Bader Ginsburg

THE RIGHT CHOICE WON'T ALWAYS BE THE POPULAR CHOICE

Being a badass means that sometimes, even when you're doing the right thing, there's a chance you're gonna be misunderstood at best, disliked at worst. Buffy knows this all too well. For starters, she's always on the hit list of the school authorities.

WILLOW: There is one name that keeps getting spit out. Aggressive behavior, run-ins with authority, about a screenful of violent incidents . . .

BUFFY: Okay, most of those weren't my fault.

—"Phases"

Poor Buffy. Even werewolf searches somehow lead to her and her problem-child rep.

WITH GREAT POWER COMES GREAT RESPONSIBILITY

And yes, that one comes from *another* superhero canon. But Buffy knows: being the Slayer is a privilege and a burden. It's not to be abused. This attitude flies in direct contrast to Faith's approach to life as a Slayer: "We don't need the law. We *are* the law."

FAITH: We *are* better. That's right. Better. People need us to survive. In the balance? Nobody's gonna cry over some random bystander who got caught in the crossfire.

BUFFY: I am.

—"Consequences"

Being Slayer—being strong—doesn't give a girl the right to abuse those less powerful. It's a duty, not a reward.

BE THE BOSS OF YOU

WESLEY: Are you not used to being given orders?

BUFFY: Giles always says "please" when he sends me on a mission. And afterwards, he gives me a cookie.

—"Bad Girls"

Buffy's gracious enough about Giles's requests, but as she matures, she realizes that 99 percent of the time, Slayer knows best. Ultimately, she quits the Council. #girlboss, amiright?

"We come in peace,
but we mean business."

—Janelle Monáe

Conclusion

Buffy herself introduces season seven of her groundbreaking series with the assertion that "It's about power." Specifically, she's talking about her slaying powers and the forces of evil generally wanting to defeat her. It's safe to say most of us can't relate to that experience *exactly*. But the show, the character, the world Joss built? That's a different story.

Buffy is nothing if not a protracted (occasionally myopic but no less enervating) metaphor for those of us struggling with the monstrosities of human life—that is to say, *all* of us. And while *Buffy* (somewhat ironically) may have been the brainchild of a white guy, consider the first image that springs to mind when the show is mentioned: Sarah Michelle Gellar, steely-eyed and holding a stake. Powerful to her core.

It's no understatement to say that regardless of who birthed the show, it's the babes of Buffy who run away with its relevance and resonance. Now let's follow these ladies' lead, take a page from their book, and go forth and slay.

"I love to see a young girl go out and grab the world by the lapels. Life's a bitch. You've got to go out and kick ass."

—Maya Angelou

The Slayer's Watchlist

Where to Find More Buffy-esque Badassery

If the Final Girl paved the way for the Buffster, then Buffy took that mantle and made it her own. She's the original-flavor vampire Slayer; accept no imitations.

But while we're eagerly awaiting more *Buffy* programming, lit, and comic fun, the show itself spawned a huge crop of worthy successors (some direct, some indirect—all fab and worth a look, especially if you've exhausted your Buffy binge).

Charmed

The sisters Halliwell practiced witchcraft and battled baddies. They looked good and traded snarky comments while doing it, too (sound familiar?). The original show aired in 1998; there's a reboot airing on the CW as of 2018.

Roswell

Another supernatural teen drama (based on a young adult book series) centered around aliens living with social alienation (get it?) in the eponymous town. It debuted in 1999 and, since everything old is new again, it's been rebooted for 2019.

Veronica Mars

Is it a stretch to call a sarcastic, mystery-solving blonde the second coming of Buffy? Okay, so Veronica Mars doesn't fight demons, but she kicks ass. The show premiered in 2004; and as of October 2018, a new season had been ordered by Hulu. Thank the gods of streaming services.

Alias

Sydney Bristol was older than Buffy when she was called to her mission, but it's worth mentioning that strong women slid into home (and lead roles) in the immediate aftermath of Buffy.

Twilight

Would there be a Bella if there'd never been a Buffy? Hard to say. The first *Twilight* novel was published in 2005, just two years after the final season of *Buffy*.

The Vampire Diaries

Buffy begets Bella, and soon after *Buffy* ended, this show debuted based on the popular young adult book series of the same name. If you liked Angel, you'll *love* Stefan. And if Spike's more your type, there's always Damon.

The Hunger Games

Buffy aired its season finale in 2003. The first novel in the *Hunger Games* trilogy was published in 2008. We're not saying there was a Buffy-shaped hole in the postapocalyptic fictive universe . . . Oh, wait. That's exactly what we're saying.

Jessica Jones

Would networks have bought that audiences were ready (and willing, and able) to watch a drama about a flawed, tough, complicated female superhero if Buffy and *Buffy* hadn't blazed the trail? To quote our fave series, "Not on the likely."

The Force Awakens

Think about it: Rey is an ordinary girl who learns that she's harboring secret powers and an unbelievable birthright.

Sure, Leia was #goals, a princess, a warrior, and eventually a general. But it wasn't until 2015 that Lucasfilm centered a film around a female Jedi. You do the math.

The fact is, there's no shortage of successors to the *Buffy* throne. She didn't just open the doors; she blew them down, and this is an incomprehensive list of the characters and shows she most definitely influenced.

BEYOND *BUFFY*

WHERE (ELSE) TO FIND YOUR FAVE BADASS BABES

The original series may be over, but these women have slayed it left, right, and center for just about forever. A boss bitch knows how to diversify, and these women make it work.

Sarah Michelle Gellar (Buffy)

Obviously, SMG will always and forever be Buffy in our hearts and minds, but this take-charge gal has been acting since she was a child and always has about a zillion irons in the fire (give or take). If TV's your thing, you can catch her on *The Crazy Ones* and *The Ringer*. Following in the Slayer's horror footsteps, she starred in the J-horror hit *The Grudge*. But more recently, she's taken a page from Buffy's book regarding our favorite Slayer's love of snacking and launched Foodstirs, a company dedicated to providing family-friendly boxed baking products that use natural, organic ingredients. As Dawn might say, "Mmm, cookies!"

Alyson Hannigan (Willow)

"Just Willow" went on to charm viewers as Lily Aldrin on *How I Met Your Mother*, starring in more than two hundred episodes. So if you're missing her on your small screen, that's a good place to start. And tapping into Willow's love of magic, she currently hosts *Penn and Teller: Fool Us*, a magic-based reality competition show on the CW. As of October 2018, the show was renewed for a sixth season.

Charisma Carpenter (Cordelia)

Queen C had a recurring role on both the original series of *Charmed* and *Veronica Mars*, two programs that Buffy fans love. And, of course, if you miss Cordelia in particular, may we introduce you to a little spin-off called *Angel*? Carpenter is also not afraid to get meta, referencing her *Buffy* beginnings while playing Chanel #2's (played by Ariana Grande) mother on *Scream Queens*.

Michelle Trachtenberg (Dawn)

If *Buffy*'s a little too intense for the kiddos, why not introduce the littlest feminist in your life to Dawn via the 1996 movie *Harriet the Spy*? (Pro tip: check out the original book by Louise Fitzhugh, too.) And when your small human is old enough, check out Trachtenberg's role as Georgina Sparks on the decidedly PG-13 series *Gossip Girl* (also based on a fantastic, compulsive book series featuring all sorts of deliciously wicked young women, authored by Cecily von Ziegesar).

Amber Benson (Tara)

The cast of *Buffy* are no strangers to comic fandom, and Benson has perhaps embraced that role better than any of her cohorts. While she's still acting and directing, she's also been very busy writing *The Ghosts of Albion*, an animated web series for the BBC, with Christopher Golden, as well as books based on the web series for Random House. Solo novels *Death's Daughter* (Penguin) and *The New Newbridge Academy* (Simon and Schuster) followed soon after. Turns out Willow was *so* right: (book) nerds are *so* in.

Eliza Dushku (Faith)

The Slayer's heir apparent initially won viewers over as a precocious child star in the smash hit *True Lies*. But she struck a serious cord as Faith on *Buffy* and went on to reprise the role on the spinoff *Angel*, too. She often gravitates toward playing "bad girls" (pun intended), telling *Maxim*, "It's easy to play a bad girl: You just do everything you've been told not to do, and you don't have to deal with the consequences because it's only acting."

Dushku has starred in various cult classics, like the cheerleading movie *Bring it On* and Whedon's TV series, *Dollhouse*. Most recently, she's gone back to school to study sociology, she's campaigned on behalf of presidential candidate Bernie Sanders, and she's spoken out about substance abuse and addiction on behalf of various causes. She's also come forward about her own experiences with sexual abuse in Hollywood, opening up more avenues to other young women to speak out.

ABOUT THE AUTHOR

Micol Ostow has written more than 50 works for readers of all ages, including projects based on properties like *Charmed*, *Mean Girls*, and most recently *Riverdale* and the Archie comics. In her former life as an editor, she worked on the *Buffy the Vampire Slayer* and *Angel* licenses, and in addition to an MFA in Writing from Vermont College of Fine Arts, she has an informal doctorate in all things Slayer-related. She lives in Brooklyn with her husband and two daughters who are also way too pop-culture–obsessed. Visit her online at www.micol.ostow.com.